Coastal Tales

Whittlesey Wordsmiths

Coastal Tales

Disclaimer
Apart from factual pieces, and where
historical characters are mentioned,
the stories and poems in this collection
are works of fiction
and characters therein are the invention
of the writer.
Any resemblance to actual persons,
living or dead, is coincidental,
whatever, our relatives might claim.

Copyright © Whittlesey Wordsmiths 2025

All rights reserved.
ISBN: 978-1-9168926-7-5

Coastal Tales

DEDICATION

Jan Cunningham
25 05 1944 - 28 07 2024

We, the Whittlesey Wordsmiths, would like to dedicate this collection to Jan Cunningham, a founder member of our group and a very dear friend.

Jan never seemed to realise how talented she was, despite our assurances. No doubt she would be both thrilled and slightly embarrassed by this dedication.

Although she may no longer be with us, Jan still is, and always will be, an ever-present, never-forgotten star.

Coastal Tales

Coastal Tales

CONTENTS

    Acknowledgments

1	Sands of Time	Pg 1
	Wendy Fletcher	
2	The Pool	Pg 4
	Henry Curry	
3	A Coastal Poem	Pg 12
	Hilary Woodjets	
4	Devils' Cove	Pg 14
	Eddie Morris	
5	Coast to Coast Plots	Pg 20
	Laraine Newsom	
6	A Heart for Valentine's Day	Pg 28
	Jane Pobgee	
7	Business As Usual	Pg 32
	Stephen Oliver	

Coastal Tales

8	Cubin Forest Morayshire	Pg 38
	Gwen Bunting	
9	Moving On	Pg 41
	Wendy Fetcher	
10	The Night I Walked on the Moon and saw stars under my feet.	Pg 44
	Val Fish	
11	Shell Hunt.	Pg 46
	Cathy Cade	
12	Finch by the Sea	Pg 48
	Philip Cumberland	
13	Emily's Letter	Pg 60
	Henry Curry	
14	Blue	Pg 66
	Jane Pobgee	
15	Coastal Love and Secrets	Pg 70
	Laraine Newsom	

Coastal Tales

16	The Tide is High	Pg 74
	Val Fish	
17	The Beachcomber	Pg 76
	Henry Curry	
18	Journey to a new life	Pg 83
	Gwen Bunting	
19	Sea Rescue	Pg 87
	Hilary Woodjets	
20	Bed Head	Pg.96
	Val Chapman	
21	The Shell Collector	Pg.99
	Phil Cumberland	
22	Muddy Waters	Pg.115
	Cathy Cade	
23	A Shorebird	Pg.121
	Laraine Newsom	

Coastal Tales

24	Winey the Witch goes to Covehithe	Pg.123
	Wendy Fletcher	
25	The Beach Hut	Pg127
	Gwen Bunting	
26	Sight for Sore Eyes	Pg 132
	Val Chapman	
27	Secrets of the Sea	Pg 137
	Val Fish	
28	Larry at Sea	Pg.138
	Laraine Newsom	
29	The Mary M Berkely	Pg 142
	Henry Curry	
30	Seal Skin	Pg 148
	Val Chapman	
31	The Last Laugh	Pg 152
	Hilary Woodjets	
32	A Serial Killer on Cromer Pier	Pg 161
	Henry Curry	

Coastal Tales

| 33 | Jurassic Coast | Pg 164 |

Stephen Oliver

| 34 | The Van | Pg.170 |

Jan Cunningham

Coastal Tales

ACKNOWLEDGMENTS

Thank you to all those who have made this book possible. That's all our Wordsmiths who have turned up, sometimes in appalling Fen weather, even on days when we had no nibbles to tempt them, and the heating was broken so we wrote with stiff fingers.

Thanks to all those who have re-read, re-edited and rewritten their contributions. Also, thanks to: Wendy, Val C, Val F and Hilary for their hours of proofreading.

Thanks again to group leader Henry and before him, Wendy who started Whittlesey Wordsmiths, and to Cathy who puts it all back together when it inevitably falls apart, as well as producing endless updated templates and fielding our million questions.

And, as always, thanks to our families and friends for their unfailing support and good humour, even when they were waiting to see if they would be the victim in **our next misadventure.**

1 SANDS OF TIME

Wendy Fletcher

It was the final day of the Abergavenny Sand Sculpture Festival. This was the first year it had been televised and there were mixed feelings among the competitors. Producers got in the way. Cameramen got too close. Sound engineers trailed wires, and the director interrupted concentration with loud bursts on the megaphone.

The last three days had taken their toll on Carl's sense of humour. Late night beer marathons in the local boozer, sharing stories and shorts, or sometimes shots, with the other competitors, had left him tired in the mornings; not the best start to long, hot days on the sand as each of them worked on their individual exhibits.

The prize money here was substantial and the TV coverage would raise the profile of even the runners-up, not that Carl was planning to be a runner-up. He knew he was good.

He had arrived a day later than anyone else, having got distracted by a pretty face on the train journey west, but that was a different story.

Now he had caught up and he could take time to stand back and evaluate his work. He smiled. His sculpture wasn't as big as most of the others. Some were huge, but his was good.

The scene was a nursery with a poised rocking horse and a row of watching toys. Right at the front, closest to where the judges would pass at four o'clock, was the baby. On a soft sand blanket with knees drawn up under a rounded tummy lay the tiny infant. The carefully sculpted strands of hair were brushed away from a high forehead and a snub nose. The rosebud mouth was slightly open as it slept beneath the midday sun.

Several people had stopped to take photos, and Carl had posed beside his work. He knew the open-necked shirt in a blue checked fabric would make a perfect contrast to the gold of the sand. The short sleeves showing off his tanned, muscular arms would be a hit with the viewers. Everyone liked winners to be handsome. It never did any harm to court the cameras.

Relaxing at the back of the enclosure with an ice cream in one hand, the other raised to shield his eyes from the glare, he was watching the steady rise and fall of the lapping waves thirty feet away. That was why he hadn't noticed the girl with tumbling auburn hair step up to the rope. The crowd was getting thicker now and his first glimpse of her was as she was already turning away.

It was a split-second decision. He could let her walk away into the crowd and perhaps never see her again, or he could destroy his masterpiece. He took three long strides forward and tripped over the sleeping baby. Sand flew into the crowd.

'I'm sorry, folks.' He held up an apologetic hand as he staggered to his feet but his eyes met hers and he thought he'd made the right decision.

'Sorry.' He smiled again. 'Are you OK?'

'Yes, no harm done,' she brushed the loose sand from her summer cotton dress and bare legs, 'except to someone's baby. I guess they won't be too happy with you.'

'No worries,' he assured her. 'The baby was mine. I can always have another one... I mean make another one... I mean build another one.'

She was laughing now, and he knew he'd made the right decision.

'I might get another ice cream.' He glanced at the cone sticking out of a hump of sand that had been the baby's rounded buttocks. 'That one doesn't seem to have travelled too well.'

Then, he pushed ahead, 'Would you like one?'

She nodded and he lifted the rope for her to duck underneath, adding 'Be careful. We don't want you tripping over anything.'

Just short of the ice-cream kiosk, a man stepped up to them with a clipboard.

'Ah, Carl McCarthy, isn't it?' He was looking at the board. 'I'm Henry Brown, one of the judges. I just wanted to say I'm really sorry about what happened. I'm afraid it means you are disqualified as we are past the deadline for completion. Damn shame, but we have to go by the rules. That was a lovely piece of work. Between ourselves, I'd say you had a good chance of winning. Guess it just wasn't your lucky day.'

'Oh, I don't know about that.' Carl grinned at the girl at his side. 'The day's not over yet.'

2 THE POOL

Henry Curry

Looking back now, it all seems so distant. The horror of it has begun to fade – a little. But hasn't left me completely; that dread can suddenly grip me at odd times. I still shiver when I see deep water, and I can no longer visit… well, some local places. And now, here I am, relating that same nightmare.

It started innocuously enough, a few years ago, when my wife and I were fortunate enough to be invited to a friend's villa, on a small Greek island in the Ionian Sea. Geoffrey and his wife Pauline are a charming couple, very old school and polite, robustly British but liberal in their thinking. Having to visit the UK on business, they invited us out for a couple of weeks to look after the place while they were away. With no particular plans for that time, we jumped at the chance of this unexpected holiday.

So there we were, little hire car parked jauntily on the dusty drive, opening the big metal doors to the house and wheeling luggage into the spacious lobby. We'd heard all about the place from them, of course, but never been before. Geoff had spent considerable time, cost, and effort with local builders to refurbish the old place that had been on the site. Pauline was a whizz of a project manager, cajoling and coaxing sensible deadlines from the relaxed craftspeople. And the result, eventually, was a fascinating mixture of a property – smart, modern facilities inside, but the exterior, an original, rustic, local farmhouse. There was everything you could wish for in a home, and we looked around the amazing lounge with its colourful paintings and modern sculptures.

I was still running my hands along the beautiful stone surfaces, but Lou quickly began to busy herself unpacking all the important stuff, so I went back to bringing in cases, bags and boxes.

"Not there, dopey, that's food. Put it in the kitchen." I picked up the bag again with mock dismay, and then blew her a theatrical kiss. "Later," she whispered, winking.

By the time we'd finished getting most of our things put away, around five o'clock, it was still a deliciously sunny afternoon with a mild north-westerly breeze keeping the day from feeling too hot. So we decided to try out the amazing swimming pool. Under an opulent sky of lapis lazuli, we swam deliciously in the sparkling, icy water, splashing and laughing like teenagers.

Drying ourselves in the hot Mediterranean sun felt very good after the cold shock of our dip. Rubbing the towel over my head I suddenly caught sight of something in my peripheral vision.

"What's that?" Staring hard toward the far end, the deepest part, I realised my voice must have sounded strange, alarmed. The look on Lou's face was odd.

"What's what?" She'd turned and was trying to follow my gaze. I was unsure – a flicker of a dark shape, something swimming.

But there was nothing there.

"Oh, I just... Well, I thought..." Staccato, unended sentences that must have been annoying. "Something down there, in the water. I don't know. I can't see anything now, though."

"Remind me not to call you as a star witness," she laughed. "Probably more leaves blowing off that sycamore. It must keep the pool man in permanent employment." She was right. Huge, dark shapes continually drifted down whenever the breeze picked up, which it did frequently. The leaves were mostly shades of brown but looked black, as they sank and appeared to move jerkily to the bottom. Yes, that was it. Leaves; just leaves. Amazing how good peripheral vision is, I told myself. Ancient adaptation, to avoid danger; stop predators sneaking up on you. Yes.

After a quick meal and a couple of glasses of wine we went to bed fairly early, tired from the journey. We hugged and kissed goodnight, the comfy king-sized double bed enfolding us, all intertwined arms and legs, as we quickly drifted off to sleep.

I was lying awake, I guessed around one o'clock, and silently got up go to the bathroom. As I walked back, I couldn't help a quick glance out of the balcony window. The pool lights were still on. An automatic timer I guessed – no – hoped. Had I switched them on by mistake? And now they'd be on all night.

I didn't want to break out of my warm drowsiness and traipse downstairs to check. All was beautiful, shimmering blue, glassy water, just occasional ripples from the wind. But no – what was that? I didn't have my specs on. I was sure there was some sort of dark shape in the water. I involuntarily shivered. Not leaves, no. This was moving purposefully. Swimming.

I was fully awake now, alert, adrenalin pumping. I went down the cool stone stairs to the kitchen and found a torch. I was spooked but had to investigate. Was some animal in the swimming pool? I opened the French doors, and as I did so a dark shape emerged from the pool and slithered towards me. I tried to scream...

"Hey, hey, there now, shh." Lou was hugging me. "Just a nightmare, you're okay."

I was sweating and sitting up in bed. Apparently, I'd shouted out; one of those things you do in bad dreams to wake yourself up before the evil thing you're dreading gets you.

"Wow, sorry honey. That was all so vivid, so real." Ever since the accident I'd had the occasional nightmare, so we're kind of used to it. Still, my heart was pounding.

"Come on, let's get back to sleep. Be brave, my soldier," she gently teased as she cuddled me. All seemed better. I heard Lou's soft breathing and I eventually got back to sleep.

I woke around seven-thirty, quite late for me; I'm normally an early bird. Louise had been up for ages, bustling with breakfast, looking at maps, and planning the day.

I showered and got into shorts and tee shirt, helping Lou take all the things for breakfast out on the patio. We ate peaches that seemed the size of small cannon balls, soft bread rolls from the local bakery, honey and yoghurt, and gallons of fresh coffee. I was relaxed, ready to face the day. Lou looked and smelt gorgeous. We soon took ourselves off for a long walk and sat under the shade of a jacaranda tree as the sun climbed to the zenith. To quote the brochures, it really was quite idyllic.

Lunch in a local restaurant was relaxed and unhurried. It was just turning to a beautiful sunset as we got back to the villa. Its friendly yellow stone walls were aglow in the evening light. Was it too late for another dip in our pool?

"You go ahead, I'm a bit tired." Lou looked dark under the eyes; I totally understood. But it was still warm, so a quick swim in the blue water was inviting.

"Okay honey, you relax. I'll fix us a drink and a snack after I've showered and changed."

I crossed the stone flags and bent down to put my hand in the water, testing the temperature, as you do. A dark shape seemed to flit across the tiles at the deep end. I wasn't fazed this time – just more leaves swirling around. I stepped into the chilly liquid and winced as it contacted my nether regions. No place for wimps – I jumped straight in and started to swim a leisurely crawl to the far end.

Just as I made to turn, something slimy touched my foot. I automatically kicked out and tried to swim away, but now I was being held fast, one leg clamped by whatever it was. I'm a confident swimmer but I admit I panicked – what the hell was doing this? I couldn't shake it off. Then things went from bad to worse. I was being dragged down under the water.

I splashed, shouted and began to choke, but I could feel myself being pulled right down, towards the deepest part. Right to the bottom. My eyes were open as I struggled to free myself, kicking furiously. And I could see the black shape, a hideous outline.

I must have lost consciousness.

A bright light in my eyes, a painful glare, woke me. I coughed and tried to sit up.

"Take it easy. No rush, take your time." Lou was fussing over me at the side of the bed. I gradually took in the scene; the odour of disinfectant, the rhythmic noises, machines and alarms pinging. I realised this must be a clinic or hospital of some sort.

"The doctor said you should be okay to go home soon. It's lucky Georgios came by and heard you when he did." She leant and kissed me.

"Heard me? What happened, why am I stuck in here?"

I was confused and restless, wanted to get up. Who was Georgios?

"You were in the pool, had gone for a swim. But something must have happened – we're not sure what. Maybe you bumped your head. You were struggling down in the deep end. The pool man Georgios happened to be passing, saw you and pulled you out."

Strange flashes began to pop into my mind – I could see the dark shape again. I could feel the slimy thing gripping me, holding my foot. I felt the choking, as I was thrashing in the water.

"My god, it sounds as though this Georgios deserves my thanks for saving me!"

I didn't mention the black thing, the grip that pulled me down. Not yet.

"Well, I called an ambulance right away and here you are. But the odd thing is, Georgios went off straight after. I called Pauline in London to try and find out his details, where he lives, but she said they'd never heard of him. The guy who looks after the pool for Geoff is called Dimitrios and he is away at the moment."

As Lou spoke, my head was fuzzy, and I couldn't make sense of things. I determined to check a few things out.

Later, back at the villa, I rang Geoff. With the doors shut and the curtains drawn.

"What can you tell me about the background to this place Geoff?"

He gave me lots of building and practical information, before he went on to describe the history.

"Well, the old farmhouse adjoined what was called Diabolos Fields. People hereabouts said the land was an old cemetery or something and was bad. Cursed. I thought it was just local nonsense."

He laughed, uneasily. "I bought it up rather cheaply and recently had the pool built on it. But a guest staying a couple of months back said he thought he'd seen a strange dark shape in the water – came out in a right state. I thought it must have been the drink – old Barry can put it away – but he's a bit highly strung. Now I'm not so sure. Pauline and I have lately been a bit wary of using it; we won't go near it now!"

"Okay to let us discover whatever the problem may be for ourselves!" I chuckled.

"No, not at all. We just didn't want to spook you with mysterious apparitions and the like. Things that are probably just in susceptible people's imagination. Maybe we should have told you. Anyway, I'm pleased you're okay now. Did they say why you had your funny turn in the water?"

I opened up, told Geoff about my experience, about the dark shape and the thing gripping me.

"My god, I'm so sorry. Maybe it's time we took this a bit more seriously."

There was a note of anxiety in Geoff's voice.

"I haven't told Lou yet, best keep it that way till we know more. She thinks I have a bit too vivid an imagination as it is. And there's another thing…."

I was puzzled about my erstwhile saviour, the man nobody knew or had heard of. "Who was this Georgios who just happened to be in the right place at the right time?"

"Georgios? Did you say Georgios?" Geoff's voice rose.

"Yes, that's who Lou said pulled me from the pool. Pauline said you didn't know him."

"The local church is Saint Georgios. He's the Patron Saint of water."

3 A COASTAL POEM

Hilary Woodjets

The Northeast Coast is spectacular.
"Bloody gorgeous," in the vernacular.

Castles in plenty with gory tales to tell
The Border Riever thieves often gave them hell.

But it's home to many stalwarts
on which our history's founded,
They come to see where heroes lived,
and what made them so grounded.

There's Mr Brown whose gardens graced
many a stately home;
His 'Capability' in landscaping
got him very well known.

And Grace became the Darling
of the nation when she saved
many, with her father,
from the sea's quite brutal waves.

Coastal Tales

Armstrong built 'Cragside,'
lit with hydro electric power,
A scientist, inventor, engineer;
a real man of the hour.

Thomas Bewick, wood block maker,
loved illustrating British Birds
Bewick's Swan's named after him,
an honour he deserved.

All these people, and several more,
found their inspiration
Along the coast and countryside,
its glories in profusion.

4 DEVIL'S COVE

Eddie Morris

Jessop heard a strange noise emanating from inside the old cottage as he inserted a large key to open the rickety door. It was a sound he had never heard before.

The only luxury the cottage possessed was a single large cold water tap, there was no electricity. Jessop gingerly pushed open the old wooden door and shone his flashlight round the dark damp room.

He felt his body shiver in the atmosphere, although the room would soon warm up when he made a fire in the large ancient log burner. He decided to check the one room upstairs, just to make sure vermin hadn't made their way into the cottage. That might have explained the weird noises he'd heard, but everything seemed fine.

He made his way down the steep narrow stairs, went outside to the log store and gathered an armful of logs. As he was doing so, he glanced over to his only neighbour who lived in the other fisherman's cottage, about ninety metres from him. The couple who lived there were environmentalists in whose company he had spent many a pleasant evening, always with plenty of wine and conversation. They had electricity provided by a generator. After a very expensive divorce he couldn't afford a generator. The fishermen and their families who lived in these two cottages must have had a very tough life with no amenities to make their lives easier.

The sun started to sink below the horizon, its dying rays reflecting off the sea. Jessop liked the feeling of being cut off from the madness and noise of the city. It meant he could concentrate without interference on his novel.

As the sun set below the horizon, darkness descended onto the cottage, and Jessop realised he had mislaid his torch. The room being pitch black would make finding his matches and candle, or indeed his oil lamp, almost impossible. He crawled through the entrance onto a cold stone floor.

He moved around the small room feeling with his fingers everywhere for a candle and matches. Then the weird noises started again.

Jessop's hands were shaking uncontrollably. With a sigh of relief he located the items. Fumbling with the matches and candle, he managed to light the wick. The weird screeching became high-pitched and more intense, which made him dizzy and nauseous.

"Come on you idiot; it's probably something and nothing," he said to himself.

With the light of the candle he found the oil lamp, much to his relief. Jessop looked at the large wood burner.

"That's where the commotion's coming from," he said. He could see ash and large black feathers round the front of the log burner, which was in need of some repairs. He found some tools which would help him dismantle the unit then set to work.

"I don't need this distraction when I have a deadline to meet with the editor and printers," he muttered.

Jessop toiled for a good three hours to dismantle the rusting unit. Finally, the last stubborn part was ready to be removed. By now he was covered in old grease and soot, with cuts to his hands and part of his right arm, caused while struggling to loosen rusting bolts and metal. He decided a fortifying drink before the final hurdle would be a good idea. He found a bottle containing a small amount of Drambuie, his favourite drink.

"This will do fine" he said in a loud voice as he sat on a stool to savour his amber nectar. While enjoying his whisky he moved to a much more comfortable chair and promptly fell into a deep sleep.

He was jolted suddenly out of his sleep by wild wailing. He was cold although sweating profusely and his clothing hung from his body, dripping and leaving a puddle beneath his chair.

The room became eerily still, although he could hear the sound of laboured breathing. He ran up the narrow stairs into the bedroom, pulled off his wet clothes, grabbed a towel and dried himself down.

Now, dressed in fresh clothes he stood looking at what was left of the log burner. He moved cautiously towards the dark opening and lowered himself down onto his knees.

A pair of red glowing eyes were staring back at him. He crawled further into the cavity, and then the panic set in. He tried to shuffle backwards but whatever was staring at him moved even closer.

A piercing scream terrified Jessop so much, he lost control of all his bodily functions. He couldn't turn to get out with the entrance being too narrow. He peered through the dark void, his eyes bulging with fear.

Out of the darkness two large blackened hands wrapped themselves round his neck like a vice and squeezed hard. He struggled to loosen their grip but they just seemed to tighten even more.

Tumbling out from the remains of the wood burner, they rolled across the stone floor, colliding with the outer door which flew open with a mighty bang. The hands round Jessop's neck became tighter to the point where he could hardly breathe. Then everything went black.

Jessop drifted away; he was losing the fight. The couple living in the cottage nearby heard the screaming and ran out to see what the commotion was all about.

They found Jessop lying on the grass with both hands round his throat. They couldn't loosen his grip.

"Quick, phone for an ambulance," the woman urged her husband. "And the police. I can't find a pulse," she shouted. "I think he's dead."

A sheet was found to cover the body out of respect while they waited for the authorities to turn up. The medics ran to where Jessop lay and pulled the sheet down to his chest. They could not believe what they saw. They tried to loosen the grip of his hands from around his throat but to no avail.

The police arrived and asked, "What have we got here?"

"Well I suppose it could be a murder," said the medics.

"Murder" the constable said "I wonder who's responsible?"

"Him! He did it!"

"Who did?" the constable asked.

"The guy under the sheet," retorted the medic.
The constable pulled the sheet down.
"Oh! I see what you mean."
While the constable and the medics were talking, Jessop's hands dropped away from his neck.
"What the hell is going on?" he asked.
The medics, recovering from the shock of seeing a man they believed dead suddenly sit up, put him on a stretcher and loaded him into the ambulance.

Twelve years had passed since the incident at the cottage and Jessop had recovered. He had been making enquiries for someone who could take him to the cottage he had once owned.
"We will see what we can do for you Jessop." The superintendent said.
After a few days he gave Jessop the good news.
"I can take you over to the cottage in the morning."
They set off for Norfolk and arrived at midday. Jessop got out of the car and walked into the field where the cottages stood. All that was left standing was the chimney, along with part of the wood burner still visible. Then Jessop could hear the shrieking and the mocking laughter again with voices telling him, "Go away! This is not your place anymore. Go away! We told you not to return."
Jessop ran to where the car would be waiting for him. The car had vanished.
"We told you not to return, you didn't listen, did you?" the sinister voice whispered in his ear.
"You should not have returned, we did warn you."
Jessop stared at where the cottage once stood shaking his head and pulling out his hair.

"Leave me alone, leave me alone," he cried. "I want to go back to the hospital; they looked after me there." Jessop sobbed.

"Jessop," the sinister voice whispered, "You belong to me now. You will wander Fisherman's Cove for eternity. This is your calling, handed down to you, which you will obey."

With those last haunting words, Jessop disappeared from mortal view. He haunts the sands of Fisherman's Cove to this day, waiting for new owners who want to live in the one and only vacant, but haunted, Fisherman's cottage.

5 COAST TO COAST PLOTS

Laraine Newsom

As Luca was walking along the coast at Skegness, he nearly tripped over someone's feet. He was just about to give the person a mouthful when he looked at the figure sitting on a bench with his feet spread out, his head in his hands. He looked like a tramp, dirty with ragged clothing. Yet there was something familiar about him.

"Antonio," Luca said in a shocked voice.

Antonio looked up and started to cry.

Luca tried to comfort his brother. They had not seen each other for sixteen years. Their parents had come to Britain from Italy when the boys were just three and two years old. They were very different, Luca noisy, always in some kind of trouble whereas Antonio was quiet and shy.

Their parents had been killed in a car crash when attending a family funeral in Italy. It was a shock; the boys at fifteen years old had become orphans. Luca became a bit wild getting into one scrap after another. Antonio had enough and, at sixteen years old, left without a word. Luca was now thirty-three and Antonio thirty-two.

Coastal Tales

Luca had rented a holiday cottage in Skegness and took his brother back there with him. His mind had already started working with a plan.

The brothers were the image of each other. Both were the same height, only Antonio was slimmer. After a shower, Antonio put on a shirt and trousers of Luca's. They were a little loose but Luca thought with a few good meals inside him he would soon fill them out.

A mobile phone rang. Luca was expecting the call.

Patricia was married to Robert Blake, a wealthy businessman with a violent temper, involved with crooked dealings. It was when Luca was involved in some shady business with Robert that he had met Patricia. She had been sporting a black eye.

Within six months he had fallen in love with her. She was scared to reveal that she felt the same way.

Robert paid well and Luca volunteered to pick Patricia up from hospital after she had fallen, cracking two ribs. This was when she opened up to Luca about her feelings for him and the abuse that was constant from her husband. She hated him, and she'd had enough.

They decided that together they would hatch a plan. He had come to Skegness where he was not known and booked the cottage to try and fathom out what to do.

"Are you alright?" Patricia asked.

"It's you I'm worried about," he answered.

"I am okay. We are going to our property in France next month; do you think we can work something out?" she asked.

"I have a plan," he answered.

Coastal Tales

Antonio at sixteen had flown to France and worked his way to Italy. He stayed with an uncle who was a chef and who taught him to cook. He worked hard and after six years the uncle made him a partner of the restaurant. They worked well together for four years before the uncle had a fatal heart attack.

Antonio was sad and lonely; he had loved his uncle. The restaurant was successful, and he managed to keep it going until a cousin he had never heard of claimed it was his.

Antonio was shocked. He told the cousin it belonged to him, and he had paper work to prove it.

A week later, during the night, the restaurant was ransacked. He told the police about the cousin but they said there was no-one of that name.

The very next day two men broke into his home and said he had to sign the restaurant over. Antonio refused so they smashed his hand with a hammer and held a gun to his head. Forced to sign, he no longer had the restaurant or the house.

His hand being severely damaged meant that he couldn't work. He used his savings to travel through Italy, Monaco and France, staying overnight at various hotels. His money did not last long.

By the time he arrived back in England he was penniless and living on the streets. He had been feeling suicidal and when he looked up and saw his brother he had cried with relief.

Listening to his brother's story saddened Luca and he promised to help him, but first he needed help himself. Luca had made a lot of money, not always legitimately. He owned pubs, clubs, taxis, houses and betting shops. He seemed to have the knack of buying at the right time for the right price. He had been lucky.

Coastal Tales

He was nicknamed Luca Locks because of his dark curly hair but this had been changed to Luca Lucks because everything seemed to turn to gold where he was involved. Because of his lifestyle he had a number of former and current gang members who would help him out. He always paid generously.

He had cut ties with Robert after he had taken Patricia home after her ribs were broken. Luca was a hard man but well liked and Robert's bodyguards were now on his payroll.

By this time, Luca's business was mostly legitimate but there was one more thing he had to do.

Luca had many friends in different professional fields, and he arranged for Antonio to see a surgeon about his hand. The surgeon advised surgery to realign the bones. It would take three or four weeks to heal, followed by several months of discomfort. Luca arranged for the surgery to be carried out.

The next stop was to Sally, who cut Antonio's hair so that he would look identical to Luca.

Antonio was to stay at the cottage and rest, while Luca drove to Chelmsford to meet up with Patricia for the next part of the plan. They made sure they were discreet and met up on the roof in a multistory car park which was left mostly empty.

Patricia gave Luca the keys to the Villa in France along with the code to disable the alarm system. He was to get there the day before Robert was due to arrive. He had less than four weeks to set everything up.

Once the plan was ready Antonia had to be seen and impersonate Luca by wearing his clothes, going to restaurants, making arrangements to view property, withdrawing money from cash machines, and phoning pre-arranged numbers of acquaintances, using Luca's phone. This would give Luca an alibi if one was needed.

Just as Luca was about to throw away Antonio's old clothes a newspaper cutting fell from the torn jacket pocket. There was a picture of a wedding celebrating the marriage of a Mr and Mrs Marino. Antonia explained that he had spotted this in a newspaper while travelling through France. Mr Marino was the fake cousin.

Everything was in place and ready.

Alain, a Frenchman who once had his life saved by Luca when they were teenagers, would do anything for Luca.

Alain arranged everything that was needed to help Luca get into France. Although there was an element of risk, for Luca, it was a chance worth taking. He was going fishing with men he felt he could trust.

In the early hours of that morning, the weather was reasonably calm. They were about to enter the French waters of the English Channel, when another boat drew up alongside, as they had planned. Luca continued his journey in a French fishing boat.

On arrival at the French coast, he was met and quickly ushered to safety.

He stayed at Alain's villa to gather his thoughts and further plan what he was intending to do. Later he was to be driven to Arras, where Robert had his luxurious villa with a pool. It was very secluded, which was going to make his job easier.

Once the daylight had gone, he was driven, with backup, to the villa. The journey took a good hour. On arrival they met with two more of their group who declared all was clear. They entered the villa, dismantled the security system and deleted any videos that could incriminate them. He would stay overnight in the villa in order to make his move on Robert the next day.

Patricia knew her husband planned to meet up with associates that were important for his business, so he would not be deterred from going. She was to fake sickness and promise to join her husband once the sickness subsided.

In order for this to work, Robert needed to arrive by early evening, as Luca needed to meet with the French fisherman again by midnight and progress to where the English fishermen would be waiting.

Luca made himself comfortable in readiness for the next day. In case of any trouble, Alain's men were close but out of sight.

When Robert still had not arrived by seven o'clock, Luca was getting concerned. He needed to use the bathroom, and it was at this very inopportune moment that he heard movement.

Robert was here; his footsteps could be heard coming up the stairs. Luca held his breath, but he heard Robert close the bedroom door. Sounds followed from the television.

Luca checked for his gun; it was now or never.

He crept towards the bedroom door and gently opened it. Robert was in a large armchair with his back to him. What shocked Luca was what was on the screen.

He felt sick.

If he had had any qualms about what he was about to do before, he had none now. Robert suddenly turned. Luca took aim and fired.

Robert was dead before he could utter a word.

Luca left the body slumped over the armchair with the television still on. He had been careful to wear gloves around the villa; every precaution had been taken. He switched the light on and off to let the two men on guard know he was ready.

Taking a last look at the screen where a young girl was being raped, he left with tears in his eyes. He would have liked to avenge his own form of punishment on the rapist, and hoped that the police would catch this animal.

The two men drove him back to Alain's where he prepared to return to the French coast and board the fishing boat.

Reliable people had been handsomely rewarded to disappear at the right time, and it was this that made their fishing trip less perilous. They left the French coast in good time. The channel was choppier than on the inward journey, but the transfer of fishing boats could not have gone better.

It was a relief to get back on the English coast; his lift was ready and waiting.

He arrived back at the cottage to hear his brother snoring.

Patricia was relieved to hear his voice. Luca was tired, but even so they were talking for at least an hour.

They would need to get rid of these burner phones; Luca's gun was already deep in the channel waters.

They would meet after the funeral in order for him to offer his condolences and would go on from there.

Luca climbed the stairs to his bedroom and fell straight to sleep, still wearing the clothes he had arrived in.

He woke to his brother's voice saying," hey who looks like a tramp now?"

Luca smiled. "We look too much alike you're going to have a haircut."

Later that day Sally came round and shaved off all of Antonio's hair, but Luca did not want to take any chances and felt that Antonio needed to be away for the time being.

Antonio had got used to a warm climate. He preferred that to chilly England but feared going back to Italy. He decided Spain would be a good alternative.

Luca had a modest property in Spain which Antonio could have as long as he wanted. Once his hand was functioning properly, Luca would buy him a restaurant. He intended to look out for his brother.

The day Luca left to go back to his home in Billericay, Antonio flew to Spain.

All Luca's businesses were now legitimate. He wanted to leave his criminal activities behind him to provide a better start for him and Patricia. He looked again at the newspaper picture of the wedding of the Marinos.

There was just one last thing he needed to sort out.

6 A HEART FOR VALENTINES DAY

Jane Pogbee

As she stood on the sand looking out to sea, she was remembering the last time she was here. Was it just two years ago that she and Sam had come to the beach?

She was so happy that he'd asked her to join him that Valentine's Day. She was excited, thinking that he might have planned to surprise her with a special proposal.

They had stopped in the village for lunch that he had booked without her knowledge. She had been nervous during the meal, wondering if this was going to be 'it'. However, lunch passed with no declaration of undying love or rings hidden in her crème brûlée.

They chatted about their friends, books they'd read and all manner of things – all except their feelings. She knew she was in love with him and was sure he loved her too.

Afterwards he had suggested a walk on the beach, and she was happy to indulge him. The weather was surprisingly mellow for February. They were walking arm in arm at the water's edge when he broke away suddenly and using a piece of driftwood drew a large heart in the wet sand and then drew both their initials inside it.

He laughed as a wave rolled in and covered the heart, when it rolled back the heart was gone. She let out a small sigh of sadness, but he laughed out loud again.

"That's life" he said, "one minute there, then it's gone, but we have the memories." He took her in his arms and kissed her tenderly.

With his arms still holding her close he said "I'll always remember you, you're etched on my heart. I'm going to miss you."

"What?" she said. "What do you mean, you'll miss me?"

He held her at arm's length and explained how he'd had an amazing job offer and had already accepted it; he would be leaving for America in just over a week. Her mouth fell open and she felt weak.

He was going on and on about how it was the opportunity of a lifetime, and he was so glad it had happened while he was still young and not tied down.

Taking a deep breath she tried to steady herself and take in what he had said, but she blurted out "What about us?"

He stopped speaking and took a step backwards, with a surprised look on his face.

"Look, we've had a great time, but we both knew it wasn't forever. We've had fun and I'll always have the most wonderful memories of our time together. But I've got to go where the work is."

Her face almost crumbled, but her pride made her hold it together. She wanted to scream and shout why can't I come too, we're good together, we could make it work.

She didn't, she managed to smile and, "Sure, it's been fun and I'll miss you for a while...".

She saw his face light up with relief and he hugged her again and began telling her all about the new job, how wonderful it would be.

A large wave brought her back from the past as she scrambled away from the water's edge.

She had nursed her broken heart for six long months, then given herself a good talking to and decided to get on with life. So here she was two years later wandering along the beach on Valentine's Day.

She glanced around and saw Sam running towards her with a heart-shaped balloon. He reached her, went down on one knee and producing a ring from his pocket, proposed to her.

Once she had given her answer, a resounding "Yes," he scooped her up in his arms kissing her face all over.

He had told her it was only fitting that he propose here on this very same beach where he had made the biggest mistake of his life.

He had gone to America full of hope and dreams but in just a few short months, realised he had made a huge mistake. He hated the fast-paced workaholic culture, the food, the cost of everything.

Most of all he hated the fact that he was missing Sarah. He missed talking with her, her smile, how she always could make him laugh when he was feeling down. He missed how she always smelled so fresh and clean, how she would laugh with her whole body. He realised he was missing her love.

He finally realised he couldn't just live with memories of her and high tailed it home to tell her so.

It took a long while before she would give him the time of day. She was quite cold at first, but eventually he wore her down and she agreed to go out to dinner with him.

The rest was history; a slow growing realisation that she still loved him as he loved her.

He still had to prove himself to her – prove that he wouldn't disappear at the drop of a hat and that he would never leave her again.

Finally, he convinced her and today was the start of the rest of their life together. He drew a big heart in the sand, included their initials and told her that it was above the water line and could never be washed away. It would, like his love, last forever.

7 BUSINESS AS USUAL

Stephen Oliver

Matthew Tyler glanced at his friend and business partner, 'Slippery' Sid Symes.

"Can we still do our regular 'special' work," he asked, "now the Germans have occupied Jersey?"

"Sure," Sid replied.

"Are you? I mean, the Krauts will be on the lookout for anything suspicious in the waters in case England decides to take us back again."

"I can guarantee I'll get the goods in on time."

"Then I can put the advert in the local paper?"

"Sure."

As always, Matthew wondered which God was responsible for Sid's looks whenever he looked at his friend. His long face had a greenish-white hue, his eyes bulged, he had no lips to speak of, and the edges of his ears looked scalloped. Odd folds ran down his neck.

The next day, July 2nd, 1940, the German commander's orders to the island's citizens were the only item on the front page of The Evening Gazette.

Matthew's advert on the back page read, "Business as Usual." For most people, including the German occupiers, this meant that the company would continue to sell its household goods, preserved foods, and fresh produce as usual.

For those in the know, it meant that their smuggling operation, bringing 'specialized' goods to the island, would also continue.

As soon as the shop opened, the usual flow of housewives and bachelors began: Mrs Boggins asking for the three sausages for her husband's breakfast; Jimmy Jones wanting milk for his porridge, Farmer Millikan bringing the latest batch of fresh eggs from his brood.

"I'm sorry, there are only a dozen eggs," he said to Matthew when he came in. "These are from Maisie and the other late layers. The Germans took the rest."

Matthew nodded.

That was to be expected.

The first of the 'special' requests didn't come in until after lunch when Giles Penrith sauntered in.

"Any snuff available?" he asked with a raised eyebrow.

Matthew shook his head.

"Sorry, not today. Try again Friday."

"Ah, well," Giles said. "I suppose I'll have to wait."

He strolled out again.

Matthew made a note on a small pad behind the counter: Penrith: cocaine.

Later, he added more entries: Mrs Rogers's silk stockings, Smithers's single malt scotch, and Dr Morgan's penicillin.

He smiled as he wrote the last one down, remembering the day he and Sid had rescued an army medic who had almost drowned while fishing on holiday. He would never have been found had they not spotted his sinking dinghy. In gratitude, he supplied them every so often with penicillin filched from army supplies. Now, things might get a little dicey since the Allies' rules forbade any information about penicillin from international communications. Hence, their black-market supply might be endangered.

Fortunately, none of the items was particularly large, so Sid could make the trip in his tiny boat instead of using Matthew's larger one.

That evening, they sneaked down to the secret bay, where they kept their boats.

Sid untied his tiny craft and stepped in, pushing off and paddling out into the sea. It would be quite a while before he could start the engine.

Matthew shaded his eyes and watched for some time as it disappeared into the distance before making his way back home.

Sid wouldn't be returning until the following night.

Matthew was forced to tell several of his 'special' customers the following morning, "Sorry, not until next week. I can take your orders, but we're already taking deliveries."

They knew Sid was already underway and wouldn't be going out again for several days. It would be too dangerous to try too often.

Once, it had been the Coast Guard and Customs officers he had to worry about; now, it was the Germans.

As soon as he closed the shop, Matthew made his way to the bay and commenced staring out to sea.

The sun had almost set before he saw the tiny shape out on the waters, slowly approaching him.

It had almost reached the shore and the secret bay when a roar announced the approach of a German gunboat bristling with weapons and soldiers coming around the headland. It was evident they'd been waiting for him and didn't want him to escape back to sea.

Someone shouted German at the figure in the little craft as a roving spotlight speared it.

The person stiffened for a moment, then grabbed a large package and leapt over the side into the water.

The German boat opened fire, hitting the little ship multiple times until it blew up as something hit the fuel supply.

"Sid!" Matthew gasped.

Despite the explosion, the Germans continued to pepper the water with bullets, no doubt hoping to catch the swimmer as they came to the surface, without success.

Nobody came up for air. No corpse floated up.

Matthew continued to stare at the burning wreckage, his heart aching for his friend.

A splashing sound on the rocks below drew his attention away from the scene.

Sid climbed onto land, dragging behind him the package he'd grabbed as he leapt into the water.

"What the Hell?" Matthew shouted, then clamped his hand over his mouth to avoid attracting the attention of the Germans.

"I'm sorry I'm late," Sid said. "As you can see, I ran into a little trouble. They must have spotted me somehow."

"But how on Earth did you escape?" Matthew asked as he helped carry the package up the slope to their waiting car.

"I took a deep breath and went deep to avoid their bullets."

"How long did you have to hold your breath?"

Sid shrugged.

"Not as long as you think."

They took the haul back to the shop, hid the items among the rest of their goods, and then headed off to celebrate after Sid changed out of his sodden clothing.

Today, Matthew decided to ask Sid some direct questions while they drank in their usual corner of the pub.

"Sid, I know it's kind of personal, but how come you look the way you do? And how can you hold your breath for so long? It's as if a fish or a frog mated with your ma."

Sid gave him a sideways glance as he took a sip from his beer before answering.

"It was grandma, actually."

"What? You mean something…?"

"Yes. They're called the 'Deep Ones'."

"Deep Ones?"

"Yes. They're creatures from the deepest parts of the oceans that can survive at any depth."

"Oh," Matthew paused momentarily as he tried to understand the implications. "And they mate with humans? Why?"

"Survival. If they don't have fresh blood from time to time, they start losing their intelligence and become nothing more than dumb creatures."

Matthew took another sip of his beer.

"Are there any advantages of being a half Deep One?"

"Apparently, we live a bit longer than humans. In a couple of decades, I'm told, I'll change and will want to spend all my time in the water. It is, after all, their true environment."

"How did it help you swim out of danger from the Germans, though?"

"Ah, that's the best part." The folds in his neck seemed to flex and change as he rubbed his hands over them. "These are gills. They let me breathe underwater."

"Thank God for that," Matthew laughed.

"Their God is called Dagon," Sid replied. "He's the true God of the seas, the one from whom I have my God-given abilities."

The following day, the shop was running business as usual.

8 CUBIN FOREST MORAYSHIRE

Gwen Bunting

On a spring day early in March, the young family decided to have a Sunday trip out to a nearby forest.

The weather was good, considering the time of year and geological area. Miles of forest lined the roads around Morayshire, reminding them of their holiday in Canada when at any moment a Moose might run across the road. There were only deer to watch out for here in Scotland.

With water bottles and a flask plus a few light snacks, the family emerged from the car which was neatly parked close to the gated entrance. Their dog, tugging at his lead, desperate for release to investigate the smells in this new place.

The boys, Craig and Neil were aged seven and four Craig the older of the two. Their dog, a mongrel with a thick wiry ginger coat, was a rescue dog which their mother had acquired before her marriage. Rakker, the dog had accepted the boys when they came into the family, which was fortunate as it would have been hard to find him a new home.

The family were well wrapped up against the weather, wearing Wellington boots and heavy coats to keep out the cold. They entered the wood, the dog bounding ahead as usual.

Coastal Tales

Through the woods they would soon reach the Moray Firth, an inlet from the North Sea. It was tidal; the flotsam and jetsam thrown up on to the beach was vast and amazing.

They reached the coast and before them piled high on the beach were all kinds of debris, ropes, fishing nets, helmets from the workers on the North Sea Gas and Oil rigs which had fallen into the water. There was some lovely driftwood, a root of some kind that intrigued them. They put this to one side just in case they wanted to carry this rather heavy piece of driftwood home.

As you may guess there were no other people taking a stroll, just this small family. The father charged off to see what he could find, like a born scavenger. The dog chased after him, the younger boy Neil holding on to mum's hand. Climbing over the rough terrain was hard work for little legs. Craig, just like his father, went exploring.

Their pile of treasure was increasing. The fishing nets still had large green balls attached, as these made them float. A few dead fish were lying amongst the rubbish, but they would be washed back into the sea when the tide turned.

Suddenly, they realised the tide was coming in rapidly, and their escape route was being enveloped by the sea. Quickly, Dad took control, picked up Neil, and grabbed Craig's hand.

They headed for the high mound of waste the sea had deposited on the beach.

Struggling to get over to the trees and forest area, Mum was left calling for the dog, looking frantically to where she thought he was.

Coastal Tales

Just ahead of her she spotted his ginger head bobbing between the waves making for dry land. She hurried to go to the higher ground and with the aid of some driftwood she managed to get to safety on the edge of the forest.

Finally, the family reunited in the middle of the wood, finding the picnic which they had hidden in some undergrowth. They were so grateful for the hot coffee and soft drinks for the boys. Soon they were munching on egg sandwiches and, with Rakker crunching his dog biscuit, this completed the family party which was so very nearly lost.

They visited this beach many more times, but always kept an eye on the tides, first making sure they had a current tidal map of the area. They remembered too, the day when Rakker picked up a recently felled young pine tree and tried to carry it home. It was about 4ft in length and a good mouthful for such a small dog to get hold of.

To this day the piece of driftwood adorns the staircase of the family home, reminding them of long-lost days of youth. The sons, now grown men, are making their own way on life's adventure.

9. MOVING ON

Wendy Fetcher

Caroline opened the hand gate that led from the cliff path to her grandmother's cottage and shook her head. She really must stop herself calling it Granny's cottage. Since the death of the old lady last spring, it was actually now her cottage. She had inherited it and was planning to move in shortly.

Luckily, her job as a book illustrator meant that she could work from home, whereever home happened to be, even in this isolated, windswept spot at the top of the cliffs in rural Norfolk.

So, why had she deliberated about making the move for so long?

Maybe it was because she had mixed feelings about the place. Wonderful memories of scrambling down these cliffs to the beach below on childhood holidays jostled with images of the eccentric old lady who had struggled to cope with an exuberant child.

The fact that her parents had been left enough money to live comfortably but she, the only grandchild, had been left the property, should perhaps have been enough to convince her that Granny held no grudges.

Here, in the bright light of a summer day, her fears seemed unfounded. But she knew that when night fell and the roar of the sea throwing itself at the base of the cliff disturbed her sleep, she would be haunted by the sound of Granny's scolding voice.

It wasn't that they had clashed over anything important, or at least what Caroline would have considered important.

Granny just had her own version of what was important.

Caroline walked towards the cottage with determined steps and only faltered once, as she passed the lilac bush in the corner of the garden. An image sprang to mind of her five-year-old self. She had snapped off a beautifully formed bloom and ran indoors to present it to Granny.

'Get that out of here.'

She could still see Granny's expression, a cross between anger and fear.

Caroline's five-year-old self turned to run.

On the threshold, she stopped, turned and spluttered, 'But I picked it especially for you.'

Granny's face had softened a little and her voice was kinder.

'I know you did.' But her hand was on Caroline's shoulder, guiding her firmly out of the door, still clutching the offending gift.

Only when she was safely outside, did Granny squat down to her level and say 'It's very pretty, Caroline. I can see why you chose it, but it's terribly unlucky to bring lilac indoors.'

Now, twenty years later, Caroline knew that if ever she was to find peace here she had to let go of all Granny's superstitions.

Shoes on the table, mirrors hanging opposite windows, crossed cutlery, diamond shapes in folded bed sheets, open umbrellas.

One by one, these old beliefs would have to be confronted and dismissed.

As she went into the shade of the cottage to look for a vase, she shuddered just once before seizing the secateurs and heading back out to the lilac bush, whispering 'Sorry, Granny, some things just have to be done.'

10 THE NIGHT I WALKED ON THE MOON AND SAW STARS UNDER MY FEET.

Val Fish

The island of Jersey is only five by nine miles, and each of its four coastlines is unique in its own way: high, rugged granite cliffs and headlands up on the North; sheltered sunny bays down at the South; the sweep of St Ouen's Bay dominating the West; and the rocky moonscape on the East.

Having visited this beautiful island for over forty years, I thought I'd seen and done it all, walked every cliff path, visited every bay, gone on all the tours.

Until I did the moonwalk!

Jersey's sea beds are covered twice a day by some of the highest tides in the world, with a tidal range of up to twelve metres. The island doubles in size at low tide.

The East coast is known for its 'lunar' landscape, the rocky seabed resembling the surface of the moon.

So on one, thankfully, dry and warm evening, three of us joined an organised group walk (known as the Moonwalk), out to Seymour Tower, just over a mile off shore, a coastal defence tower standing on a tiny island called L'Avarison.

It is not advised to do this solo; the experts know the tides and know what they are doing. I at last discovered the purpose of one the structures standing halfway to the tower. It's a safety platform for anyone who gets stranded at high tide. Which Jersey Coastguards say, happens all too often.

We explored rock pools, crossed sand bars and gullies… but the highlight for me was witnessing the bioluminescence of the marine creatures under our feet, glowing and twinkling like stars.

It is now possible to stay in the tower, let by Jersey Heritage, but if you're thinking of doing so, be prepared.

The facilities are, well… basic. A chemical toilet, no running water; drinking water is provided. No mains electricity, instead the supply is from solar power.

Your own sleeping bags and pillows have to be hauled up to the upper floor bedroom.

Worst of all, which might well put people off, including me, is you have to bag up your toilet waste on leaving and dispose of it back onshore.

I think I'll give that a miss!

It was after midnight when we turned back from the tower to head back to shore. With my favourite island in front of us and Venus shining brightly in the night sky, I walked back feeling weary but at the same time elated. It was a truly unique, magical and never to be forgotten experience.

11. SHELL HUNT

Cathy Cade

I'm searching for the perfect shell
along this stretch of beach.
Tide's out. The sea has drained away,
far as my eyes can reach.

This beach was good for finding shells;
I found my last one here.
But there were more to choose from
when I passed this way last year.

Instead, I'm finding bottle caps,
crushed cans and apple cores.
There's paper bags and plastic cups
– not what I'm looking for.

I don't need anything too big,
but larger than this one.
I don't want one too shiny
that will glisten in the sun.

I'll try those rocks below the cliff
where small sea creatures hide.
A rock pool has been left behind
on the retreating tide.

Coastal Tales

There, an abandoned whelk-like shell
looks like the very thing.
I scramble over rock.
The salty water's welcoming

It's perfect for a hermit
bound to live beside the sea
This shell's an ideal home
to suit a growing crab, like me.

12 FINCH BY THE SEA

Philip Cumberland

John Bilton stared at the metaphorical blank page, the screen of his laptop computer. He shut its lid and put on his shoes. Stepping into the hall, he donned hat and coat, intending to walk down towards the harbour. He hoped a sea breeze and salt air would clear his mind.

It was a steep descent down the cobbled street, slippery when wet, sprang to mind.

Thinking about it logically, would a walk down to the harbour of a small coastal village help with the plot of, possibly, an urban murder story? He hadn't decided the plot fully yet. Well, a walk was worth a try he thought.

The bakery was a temptation. Their jam doughnuts were the stuff of legends and a tray of them lounged provocatively in its window. However, it was a reflection in the window which surprised, well... startled him. John had last seen that figure – a man in a dark suit and a black trilby carrying a briefcase with a mackintosh folded over his arm – in his imagination, standing on the platform of Cambridge Railway station.

John turned to look at the figure reflected in the window, who was now moving away down the narrow street towards the harbour. But the street had changed. Gone were the double yellow lines and the modern street signage. The streetlights were now old-fashioned gas lights, and a black Wolseley saloon, 1950s vintage, edged its way slowly up the hill, carefully avoiding the pedestrians who shared the carriageway. There were no footpaths.

When John had left DS Dave Finch on the smoke and steam-filled platform of Cambridge station on the last written page before the block descended, it was 1957. What was he doing here at Brackney? The sound of a steam locomotive close by gave him the how. Turning back to the bakery window, the paper labels with the doughnut prices had changed to a handwritten "1d".

He turned again to look for DS Finch, only to find he had gone, as had the Wolseley, the gaslights and the old signage. The double yellow lines had reappeared.

Arriving at the harbour he noted the tide was in and the boats in the quay were afloat. The speed of the incoming tides always surprised John, even after many years living in the village. For much of the time the boats sat on the estuary bed. Then, within half an hour, the sea rushed in and they were afloat.

The glimpses of DS Dave Finch, first as a reflection in the bakery window and then walking down the cobbled street had unsettled John, as had the change in the street itself. The doughnuts had waited for him at the bakery; he bought two but paid the current price, substantially more than a penny each.

A few yards further on John unlocked the door to what had been a seaman's cottage a century or so ago, but was now his home. After hanging his coat on the rack by the door, the hat found its way onto the top of the small bookcase in the hall. Kicking off his shoes he ambled into the red brick-floored kitchen, made a cup of tea and sat at the kitchen table before opening the laptop.

John typed in the password and waited impatiently for it to load up. He clicked on the Word file marked Rose Johnson to open it but was astounded to find another few hundred words had been added since abandoning his writing for the walk.

DS Dave Finch had boarded the train at Cambridge and retraced Rose Johnson's last known, Sunday journey to Brackney. John hadn't considered this journey in the book's plot – well, not until he had seen Finch's reflection in the bakery window. He wondered why Finch would be in the village; he certainly couldn't remember writing about it.

This was the third book in the series about 1950s Detective Sergeant Dave Finch. John had got to know his creation well, or so he thought. The questions started coming: why had Rose travelled to Brackney; was she dead? if so, how did she die? and where did she die? John's writing block started to crumble as he looked for answers to the questions.

He re-read the new words he couldn't remember writing. DS Finch mentions the Wolseley he had seen – or *a* black Wolseley – making its way slowly up the hill away from the harbour. However, Dave Finch had noticed the passenger – a female passenger, who looked like, and could have been, Rose Johnson. He thought back to the brief appearance of the slowly moving car, yes Dave Finch would have had a view of the passenger; he was the same side of the road as the passenger and looking down towards the harbour. John, meanwhile, had been watching Dave Finch.

Coastal Tales

He stood up and noticed he hadn't drunk his tea, it was still warm, just, and he quickly gulped it down. These new words restarted John's thinking. He hadn't realised Rose had travelled to Brackney. Why was she here? Was she still here? Did she actually arrive and return by train or had the Wolseley collected her from Cambridge or the local station?

DS Finch decided to visit the local police station, he had made note of the Wolseley's registration number, and it wasn't a Cambridge, Huntingdonshire or Peterborough number. There wasn't a police station as such in the village, just a police house with a room to one side serving as an office. The police house was situated near the quay, the building manned by a constable, a PC Jones.

Jones was a stout, middle-aged man, standing hatless and balding behind a counter, asking how he could help. Finch showed the constable his warrant card and read out the Wolseley's registration number, asking if Jones could contact his HQ to discover the car's registered owner.

"No need for that sergeant, the car belongs to Doctor Cavendish Walker. He lives in a big house at the top end of the village."

Jones gave him the address which Finch wrote down in his notebook.

"What brings you to Brackney, Sergeant? It's a bit far from home for you, if you don't mind me saying."

Finch took the black-and-white photo from his wallet and showed it to Jones. The photograph was a portrait of a pretty, dark-haired young woman in her early twenties.

"It's a missing person enquiry – this young woman. I think she may have been in the Wolseley."

Finch was anxious to change the subject and deflected further questions from the constable, by casually mentioning, "It seems an unusual place to have a police house, Constable, right on the quay."

"Not if you knew Brackney's history. There used to be a lot of smuggling and wrecking going on around here, in times gone by."

"Wrecking?"

"The criminal element would set up false lights to lure and ground ships then go aboard and strip them of their cargoes."

"The doctor – does he have a boat?"

"He does, but it is a bit too big for Brackney. He can only take it out when there is a particularly high spring tide."

"Oh, why is that?"

"It has to clear the sand bar; it needs deeper water to manage it."

"I see. Do you know the boat's name?"

"The *Claudette*, named after his wife. She is French."

"Thank you, Jones. I would be grateful if you wouldn't repeat our conversation. Are you on duty for the rest of the day?"

"Until 8pm."

"One more thing, could you let me have the name of your Superintendent?"

"Peters. He is based in Norwich I'll give you the phone number."

"Thank you."

Finch wrote down the number in his notebook as Jones dictated it.

With that, Finch left the police house and wandered along the quay. The blue and white *Claudette* was substantially larger than the other boats that rested on the estuary bed, waiting for an incoming tide to float them off.

John was getting restless. It was a warmer day now than earlier, the sun warming things up. Another walk down to the quay, then a pint at the Sailor's Rest was in order. He was thinking about his earlier walk, keeping an eye out for DS Finch.

Finch was nowhere to be seen on the descent to the quay, but when John turned the corner towards the Sailor's Rest there, moored up at the quay, was the *Claudette*, just as Jones had described it. Finch was there too, looking around what could be seen of the vessel.

A low flying gull distracted, John, just missing him. When he looked again, Finch and the *Claudette* had disappeared.

John was unsettled. Having a character from your novel appearing and disappearing randomly was something new for him. He wondered if it was the stress of the approaching deadline for this new book that was the cause.

Putting these thoughts to one side he entered the quiet, oak beamed public bar of the Sailor's Rest. After ordering a pint of bitter he carried it to a table near a bow window overlooking the quay. Was he hoping Finch and the *Claudette* would reappear?

Finch walked up the hill into the village, away from the quay, thankful that there were very few cars sharing this narrow street. He was going to take a look at Doctor Cavendish Walker's home.

The house on Norwich Road was an imposing detached Georgian style affair set in extensive well-kept gardens. A gravel drive led to the house through a pair of impressive wrought iron gates hinged on two substantial stone pillars. The drive opened into a large circle at the front of the house, allowing cars to park there or turn around. To the left of the house was a two-storey building that had probably been stables in earlier times but was now, it seemed, a garage with living quarters above. The doctor's black Wolseley saloon was parked at the front of the house.

Finch thought he had better phone his Superintendent to apprise him of his investigations, ask for more information about the missing girl – well, young woman really – and get some instructions. Fortunately, he had passed a telephone box on Norwich Road near to the doctor's house.

He lifted the receiver and waited for the operator. He gave her – a younger, local woman, by the sound of her Norfolk accented voice – the number for Cambridge police station. He put in four pence then pressed button 'A' once the call was answered by the police station switchboard. He asked for, and was passed to Detective Superintendent Cooper. Finch gave the superintendent the telephone number of the call box so that Cooper could call him back when the fourpence ran out.

John finished his beer, had another, then started the walk home back up the hill, turning over in his mind what Finch was up to. Who knows, he thought, the words might already be waiting for him on his laptop.

However, things were pretty much as John had left them. He typed in the further details of Finch's visit to the police house on the quay, and the look at the doctor's house, picking up the story in the telephone box as Finch waited for the call from his Superintendent…

Finch's thoughts had drifted as he waited for the phone to ring, and it startled him when it did.

Detective Superintendent Cooper was a man in his fifties, missing war service because of his age and occupation. Finch's war had largely been spent in the intelligence services. When Cooper mentioned the name of Rose Johnson's employer it rang a faint bell in Finch's mind.

During the war, much of Cambridge's university population had been scattered around the country and empire. This was fortunate, because when the so-called Baedeker air raids had taken place, a lot of talent was elsewhere.

Cooper told him, The Latitude Optical Company was ostensibly an instrument-maker specialising in optical measuring instruments. However, Cooper confirmed Finch's suspicions. Instrument making wasn't all it was involved in. Hidden in plain sight sprung to mind, not an entirely unknown phenomenon in Cambridge.

Cooper continued his narrative: Rose was known to be a member of the Communist Party, selling the Daily Worker in the city centre on Saturdays.

"Hasn't this rung any alarm bells at Latitude Optical, sir?"

"Why should it, Finch? It's her spare time and you know how lefty Cambridge is."

"What is Rose's actual job, sir?"

"She is just a typist as far as I know."

"Do you think it might be an idea to search her parent's house?"

"No, I don't think it would Finch! Bob Johnson is the Lodge's Grand Master."

"Is it okay if I hang around here for another day or two? I think I might have had a sighting of Rose, and I need to follow things up."

"Very well but don't spend too long there. And find her. I - we are doing Bob a favour."

So, thought Finch, Detective Superintendent Cooper was doing Johnson a favour.

"One more question, sir, how did Johnson know his daughter was visiting Brackney?"

"She told her mother she was visiting her friend there."

"Do we know her friend's name?"

"Anne. We don't have a surname."

Finch could tell his Superintendent was irritated by his questions and, after asking him to contact Superintendent Peters in Norfolk to apprise him of the situation, he ended the call.

John was curious, what was Finch going to do next?

DS Finch's briefcase was large enough to contain a change of clothes and a shaving kit, but it was cumbersome to carry around. He headed back down to the quay and booked a room for the night at the Sailor's Rest. After unpacking his briefcase and hanging up his clean shirt, he looked out of his window which overlooked the quay. There were two men on the deck of the *Claudette*; were they readying it to sail? He wished he had asked if PC Jones knew when the next Spring tide was due.

Finch locked his room door, pocketed the key, and walked downstairs into the public bar. Before long he had the information he needed from the barman; the spring tide was expected at 1am tomorrow, Wednesday.

Finch was acting on instinct. In the past, on a number of occasions, his instincts had served him well, guiding him with his investigations and on one occasion, saving his life.

Was that really Rose in the Doctor's car? Was the *Claudette* being readied for a trip to sea, was Rose involved in something nefarious and was she going to be on the *Claudette*, if it put to sea in the early hours tomorrow?

John was intrigued; he decided he would be on the quay at 1am to experience the atmosphere at that time of the day.

He wouldn't quite see it the way Finch would have done – the lighting had changed since the 1950s – but he could still get a sense of how it would have felt: hearing the noise of the sea as it rushed in, and the creaking timbers of the boats as they lifted from the seabed. These sounds and smells would, if not the same, be similar.

At 12.30am, John was down on the quay, wrapped in a thick coat and wearing a warm woollen hat and gloves. He had tucked himself away beside the police house, able to watch both The Sailor's Rest and the quayside where he had glimpsed the *Claudette* earlier.

At 12.35 John noticed DS Finch at the door of the Sailor's Rest. He looked over to the quayside at the *Claudette* which had re-appeared. The quay was now bathed in the dim lights of the quayside gas lamps.

Finch moved into the shadows just as the Doctor's Wolseley quietly pulled onto the quay and extinguished its lights. The *Claudette* was now bobbing high in the water, lifted by the incoming tide.

John couldn't remember having been on the quayside this early in the day before. He was watching Finch from his vantage point in the shadows. The doctor (he assumed it was the doctor) climbed out of the car's driver's seat.

The doctor was a younger man than Finch imagined he would be – in his early forties as best he could tell, in the dim lamp light. He wore a dark hat and a belted overcoat against the chill early morning, Finch's raincoat wasn't so well suited to the cold air.

The whistle of a steam train broke the relative silence, startling the doctor. The back doors of the car opened. A man got out. Rose followed - it looked like Rose in the lamplight – then another man. Rose had been between them; she didn't appear to be very comfortable with the idea.

How would Finch play this? thought, John. Was he armed?

Two more black Wolseleys coasted quietly onto the quay. Their lights were extinguished, the black police signs across their radiator grills just visible in the dimness of the night. As policemen erupted from the cars a powerful searchlight on one car was switched on, shining into the eyes of the three men and Rose.

Finch emerged from his hiding place walked over to Rose and said loudly enough for John to hear, "I've come to take you home, Rose. Your mum is worried."

Then he turned to the doctor and his men.

"You are all under arrest for treason."

Once he had given them the standard caution, another man in civilian clothes climbed out of the car with the searchlight.

"Good evening, Major Peters."

"No Finch, Dave. It's Superintendent Peters now, as you know. Thanks for your call earlier, I just had time to get things organised."

The two men shook hands; they had served together during the war.

John quietly emerged from where he had watched the scene unfold and walked unseen back up the hill to his cottage, pausing just once to look back to the now deserted quay, bathed in the brighter electric lights of the present day.

The cottage was warm and, after a coffee, he was back at his laptop typing until dawn, adding the details to Finch's latest case.

It emerged that Rose had been working as a double agent. The Russians had become suspicious…

The rest of the story, and where it went from there, is in John Bilton's new book, *Finch by the Sea*.

13 EMILY'S LETTER

Henry Curry

I approached the old house on the coast with some trepidation. In the distance, the Gothic arches and dark windows lent an air of gloom about the place that only made my depression worse.

Shadows were already deepening as I reached the forbidding gates and a bell tolled in the distance, as if warning me away. But I knew I had to go forward, go into that place. I gripped the letter.

Emily had been insistent; her words came to me again and again. She had sounded so firm and final the last time we had met. We were friends, no more than friends. She made that clear.

As I kissed her on the cheek and turned to leave, I saw her smile, but there was no happiness about her countenance. No, there was something else. I had wanted to say so much, reveal my feelings for her. My true feelings. But she had seemed so resolute, and my courage had left me. Now, an unhappy year had passed.

I paused. A sea breeze shook the trees, dragging the last few leaves away to their autumnal rest. The letter seemed to weigh so heavily. I longed to stop and read it again, to ponder each word looking behind each phrase for another meaning. But, instead, I resolved to continue.

My footsteps made the gravel crunch generously, a sound which had the effect of raising my spirits a little. I stepped forward, even strode, along that long drive. I even began to whistle a tune, one that Emily used to sing, my pace in time with the music, holding my emotions back, concentrating on walking, walking.

Then the house was in front of me and I was at the great front door. I tugged sharply on the bell-pull but heard no sound. A crow called mournfully as it rowed its way across the sky, its outstretched wingtips like fingers against the twilight. I was about to try again when I heard the sound of a bolt being drawn, and the door slowly opened.

'You are expected. Follow me, sir.'

The servant had a faded air about him, as if he had been too long in a dust-filled room. His skin was as pale as the stone of the building, and he shuffled with a peculiar gait, suggestive of some illness.

'Thank you.'

I followed him into the warm hallway and immediately began to cough, I assumed as a result of the stale, stagnant air. Light seemed to penetrate but feebly, as if an unwelcome guest, hiding from all but the middle of the floor.

As my eyes became accustomed to the faint gleam from the candle borne by my guide I became aware of a number of doors and a large staircase disappearing into the reddening gloom.

'The lady will see you in here sir.'

I was shown into a room which I thought was the study, or perhaps the library. It was hard to discern the purpose of this room due to the darkness. I could see a grand desk commanding the middle, with a large high-backed chair of very old design, I fancied, given the detailed carving on its back. In the wavering shadows I could just make out tapestries on my left, and to the right a wall of what appeared to be bookshelves.

At this point the ageing servant turned to leave, and as he did so he lit candles in each of the sconces by a great mantelpiece. The light now picked out a fine long-case clock to one side of the fireplace. I resolved to examine the timepiece as far as I could, but as I moved towards it, someone else entered the room.

'Hello Jeremy.'

It was Emily, my Emily. But it was not her. The voice I heard was harsh and broken, as if emanating from a dying volcano. I turned in happy expectations, but drew back sharply at the face before me. Her eyes!

'Emily.' My voice came in a hoarse croaking sound. I held out the letter. My words failed me. She stared blankly and spoke mechanically, in a distant way.

'I knew you'd come. But many things have changed. I... I am to be married.'

The red-rimmed eyes held my gaze. There was no pleasure in her voice, only a sense of resignation. 'You should not have come here. Please go now.'

I was shocked, but tried to remain calm, measured.

'You seem unhappy Emily. Can't we talk further? As friends? I can't leave you this way, having come so far.'

I hoped she understood that I meant so much more than just my journey.

'Then stay at the Inn tonight if you wish. Come again tomorrow, in the morning, in the daylight.'

With these words she turned and walked away before I could speak.

I spent an unhappy night at the old Inn in the seaside village. The cry of the gulls haunted me, and restful sleep would not come. In my dreams I saw only vague shapes and a shadowy figure with glaring red eyes drifting through a vast library. The books were falling towards me, and there was a smell that made me choke. I was trying to speak but no sound would emanate from my throat, and the figure crackled with an eerie laughter. Another figure seemed to be present, but I couldn't see who it was. I felt hot, fearful, in a wild panic, but I didn't know why.

I woke early but felt both disturbed and tired, unrefreshed by my troubled sleep. Washing and dressing, I saw my face in the mirror. I was distressed at how old I appeared.

I resolved to make light of the last night, to enjoy a good breakfast and a brisk walk across the dunes, back to the house. I didn't want Emily to see me looking as haggard as I felt.

There seemed to be a thick sea fog settled over the valley, so my view of the house was temporarily obscured. As I turned onto the drive, a vague outline of the old walls gradually materialised. But then my heart raced – something was wrong, very wrong!

I quickened my pace, breaking into a trot, then a full-blown run. Smoke was drifted lazily up from the broken walls and crumbling ruin; a great conflagration must have taken the house! There was no roof, only charred walls and beams.

Without realising, I had started shouting as I ran. I was shouting, shouting, calling Emily's name over and over.

'Terrible. A terrible tragedy.' A bewhiskered man in a tweed jacket was looking up at the building and calling a cocker spaniel back to him.

'Here, Jack, here boy!'

I roughly grabbed this chap by the coat lapels, shouting at him.

'Where is she? What happened to Emily? Is she safe?'

He pulled back, placing his hands on my shoulders.

'Now then, now then. Calm yourself. I'm sure all that could be done was done, young fellow.' The dog returned with a piece of paper in its mouth. 'The blaze just took hold very quickly, very quickly. It started in the library by all accounts. It was burning for three days.'

These last words seemed bizarre, barely registering.

'But what happened to the people – to the lady, Emily? Where are they?'

Blood was bursting up my neck and into my head, pounding into my ears. 'Where are they?'

'Ah, now, you obviously knew the incumbents. Well,' he looked wearily at me, 'sadly no-one survived. They found the three souls yesterday, but all had perished. The lady, her husband-to-be, and the servant. All gone.'

He gave a wistful look up at the ruins. 'I am so very sorry.'

'But... but I was here yesterday. Yesterday evening. I saw them. I spoke to them. I was here. There was no fire. They were all alive!'

He leaned closely towards me and returned a puzzled, old-fashioned look.

'I can't dispute what you say you saw, or might have thought you saw my friend. The house and all its occupants, such a tragic business, were destroyed three days ago. If you were here, as you say you were, last night…'

He tailed off, frowning. Jack the spaniel snuffled at my feet, dropping Emily's letter.

14. BLUE

Jane Pobgee

I know it was a line in a Donovan song "Blue is the colour…" but I couldn't remember the rest of the words or even the tune of the song! I don't know why or where it came from, but it was in my head. When a song, tune or lyric gets in your head and just won't go away, it is known as an earworm.

Throughout the early morning it would pop up in my mind and then I started to notice the colour too. Whether it was the blue car that stopped at the zebra crossing to let me cross, or the lady in the paper shop who served me with her bright blue fingernails. By the time I got to work the colour blue was everywhere and my brain was buzzing with those four words repeating ad infinitum.

As I entered my office building a young girl in a blue dress was leaving. When I entered the lift there were two men already in it. One of them was wearing a blue shirt and the other a blue tie. What was going on?

As I exited the lift I almost fell over a package that had been left by the lift door. It had a blue wrapper. I made my way towards my office and noticed that one of the cubicles had been decorated with balloons celebrating a child's birth and yes, you guessed it, they were blue balloons for a boy.

When I finally arrived at my own office my assistant, Geraldine, brought me a cup of coffee in a blue mug. I gave her a querying look; she told me my usual red mug had been dropped and smashed just before I arrived. This was beginning to get a little unnerving, a bit spooky. Was everything going to be blue today? I began going through the post Geraldine brought in. We sat down, and I dictated a slew of answers to all the letters.

Once she had taken them away to be typed up ready for my signature, I sat back in my chair drinking my coffee in the blue mug and thinking about the lyric that was running around my mind like Usain Bolt. Was there something special about today that I was supposed to remember? Perhaps something connected to the colour blue? As hard as I tried, I could not think of anything to do with the date or the colour. I tried to put it out of my mind and got on with the day's work.

When I left the office that afternoon, I still hadn't been able to work out why those words were still in my mind. On the walk home I began to remember a bit more of the song. "Blue is the colour of the sky, in the morning when we rise."

Slowly the tune began to come back to me, and I found myself humming it as I headed towards the promenade. I loved walking beside the sea as it always seemed to blow away the cobwebs of the day, usually taking all my worries with them. I especially loved watching the sea on stormy days. The crashing of the waves, the clouds scudding by overhead were really quite something, almost liberating.

Coastal Tales

Today the sea was calm, and the sky that beautiful blue my arty friends would call 'azure'. It was so lovely to watch the waves roll lazily in and out, almost as if the sea were breathing.

I felt myself slowing my breathing to match the waves and felt a calmness settle over me. I was not sure why the sea had this effect on me, but it had always held a fascination for me since I was a little girl. I spent most of my childhood on a beach, collecting sea shells, small bits of driftwood and any treasures that the sea would deposit on the beach such as beautifully rounded and polished bits of sea glass.

Today I didn't go down on the sand, my work shoes weren't really suitable, but I stood leaning on the sea wall just relaxing and staring out in the middle distance.

Suddenly, my eyes noticed something far in the distance, what was that? A bit of the sea was darker than the rest? No, there was something moving there. As I struggled to focus, I realised I could see an arm waving from side to side. It was a person in distress.

I immediately got on my phone and looked up the number for the coastguard. I got through straight away and was able to tell them exactly where I was and where the person in distress was in relation to me. They told me they would launch a rescue immediately.

I kept my eyes on the person in distress to make sure they didn't disappear from view. After what seemed like forever, I saw a small inflatable racing towards the person. After quite a bit of moving back and forward I could see the person being pulled on board.

It was a great relief and in no time they were heading towards the beach. I took off my shoes and ran down onto the beach as I wanted to make sure the person was okay.

As I reached the shoreline a man was being helped out of the inflatable and handed a small wide dark blue paddle board. I couldn't hold back.

"Are you alright?" I asked.

He looked down at me and said he was fine. I explained that I had called the coastguard, and he shook my hand and thanked me.

He was very tall, tanned and muscular in his swimming shorts which I noted were also blue. He told me that he had been out paddle-boarding, something he was new to, had got caught in the current and was drifting further out to sea. He had unfortunately fallen off his board and lost his paddle so he was hanging on to the board for dear life and waving his arm in the hope someone would see him.

Once he had been checked over by the coastguard and given some basic safety instructions for future reference, the coastguards got back in the inflatable and went back out to sea, heading to their base.

The man introduced himself as Barry. As we walked up the beach back to the promenade, he asked me out to dinner as a thank you for possibly saving his life. Looking into his deep blue eyes how could I say no.

Especially when I heard his surname was Blue.

15. COASTAL LOVE AND SECRETS

Laraine Newsom

We often walked along the coast until we came to the Kursaal. My friends, Linda and Brenda, would excitedly run ahead shouting at me, 'Come on Sue'.

We had been friends since school. We had grown up with the smell of the sea, having all lived around Leigh-on-sea. Southend was a short distance away and was a lot more fun, especially on a Saturday when coaches arrived, often from London on a beano day out, and everyone was happy and out to have a good time.

It was on such a day that I met Peter. He was with a group of friends, so we all joined forces going on the fun fair rides. Peter seemed to like me, and we stayed together all that day.

We both loved the big dipper, which at that time was said to be the largest in the world. I can remember the ghost train and burying myself into the folds of Peter's arms. There had been an instant attraction between us and that day was the start of our journey.

Peter was in the army and would periodically go on tour duty. We always missed one another when he was away. After he had been on one tour duty he came home and we clung to one another before taking a walk along Southend pier.

He suddenly stopped and with his arm around me said, 'I love this place and I love you. Will you marry me'.

'Yes, yes and yes', I answered

He slipped a beautiful solitaire ring onto my finger, and we looked out to the sea,.

The sea was calm, glittering with bright light reflected from the rays of the sun. That moment of happiness will always be with me.

We went to a photo booth to take our picture with my hand stuck out in front showing off my lovely ring. A year later we were married and rented a flat in Southend.

We were disappointed when Peter was to go on tour to Cyprus the week before one Christmas. We had our own celebration the night before his departure. Maybe this time...

We had been invited to Brenda's wedding celebration on Christmas Eve. Brenda was my best friend, and we worked as nurses at the same hospital. I didn't really want to go without Peter but feeling sad and lonely I decided I would.

It started to snow so I took a taxi. I ended up drinking too much, it was late, and the roads were slippery, so Thomas with his ebony skin and big brown eyes took me home.

By the time spring had come I knew I was pregnant. Daffodils were growing along the walkways as I walked along the coast. Walking always helped me focus. We had so wanted a child and had been trying for five years. But my memory kept taking me back to Christmas Eve.

Thomas had been a wedding guest from America, soon to return. I did not know him, but he had seemed nice. Both drunk, we ended up in bed. This wasn't how I behaved. I prayed the baby was my husband's. I was nervous.

The sun had been shining when I wrote to Peter to tell him the news. It was another two months before I received his reply.

He wrote that my news had been delightful but that his tour had been extended and he wouldn't be home until after the birth. There was a heat wave at that time, I was uncomfortable being large with swollen feet. I wished Peter could have been with me, this had been a long tour for him.

I was relieved when the days became cooler. Trees looked picturesque, having turned red and brown. I was ready for my child and went into labour on the 26th September.

I was both excited and afraid. My daughter was born the next day. I was told she looked like me. She did not have my blue eyes but had my light brown hair. I felt immense relief.

Peter came home on a foggy afternoon six weeks later. I watched him as his blue eyes looked into her brown eyes. I saw love.

As soon as Sue had placed the baby in my arms I fell in love with her. She was mine and would always be mine. I was going to be the best father any child could have. I looked at Sue, looking at me and smiled at her. I now had two girls to love.

Sue had always been supportive of me with my army career in accepting that being in the army meant that there were times when I would be posted abroad. We were both in our twenties and had hoped for children but that had not happened.

Sue had been told by the doctor that there was no reason for her not to have children. I had been checked by the army and was told that with a low sperm count that it was unlikely that I would father a child. As the years passed I think Sue had given up on becoming a mother.

I was due to go to Cyprus just before the Christmas before our child was born. We had both been upset as I would be away for at least nine months. We made the most of the night before I left.

I had been really surprised when I received a letter from her telling me she was pregnant. I had another fertility test done and was told that it would be impossible for me to father a child.

I had never told Sue about the low sperm count. I know it was deceitful, but to tell her would make me feel a failure being unable to give her the one thing she really wanted. And I did not want to lose her.

At first, I was upset, shocked and angry. She was not the kind of girl to have loose morals. But then I got to thinking we had both behaved badly and maybe, just maybe, we could be a real family. I would keep my secret, and she could keep hers.

So I wrote and told her how happy I was.

My life felt complete with my family. The three of us would often walk along the coast, watch the seagulls flying around in hopes of food. We would walk along the pier and remember the moment Sue agreed to marry me. We were complete.

16 THE TIDE IS HIGH

Val Fish

Having lived on the island all her life, Maggie felt like she knew every inch of it: the narrowest, windiest roads, the tiniest coves, the most rugged and dangerous cliffs, the currents and the times of high tide throughout the seasons.

And not forgetting all the out-of-the-way places the tourists didn't reach.

These were all handy things to know when planning the right spot and time to commit the perfect murder. Of course, she knew there was no such thing, but at least she could shorten the odds of being caught in the act, and at the same time, increase the chances of the body being washed away right out to sea.

She didn't need to research on Google and run the risk of her browsing history being investigated; Maggie knew it all herself.

Or at least she thought she did…

Date, time and location, sorted, next on the list was how to lure her unsuspecting husband up there.

The bastard had been cheating on her, it had been going on for some time; he had no idea that she knew.

Did he really think he was that clever? Or that she was that stupid?

It was ironic really, that this particular cliff top was one they used to walk along when they first got together, not so easily accessible as some so frequented more by locals than visitors to the island.

She told him she wanted to talk, the idea being that she would feign trying to sort things out, trying to make a new start.

Suggesting one of their happier places to meet was a master-stroke. Maggie wondered what his reaction would be. Would he take this opportunity to confess? Either way, he was going to end up at the bottom of the cliff.

But for all her meticulous preparation, there was one major problem she had not envisaged; the strength needed to physically handle a man of his size.

He was six five and a hundred and sixty pounds, she half his weight, and a foot shorter, proving no match for him.

'It was such a tragic accident,' the distraught husband told reporters, 'One minute we were walking along the cliff path, the next minute she'd gone.'

They never found the body; on one of the highest tides of the year, it was quickly washed out to sea.

17 THE BEACHCOMBER

Henry Curry

Do you like walking on a beach? I suppose there aren't many people that would say no to that simple pleasure. Because, at any time of year, there's always something of interest, isn't there?

Rock pools, magically colourful pebbles, shells – even when they're broken – with those intricate shapes and weird textures. Smooth, golden sand, yielding to the pressure of your feet, with bare toes alive to the gritty softness. Leaving footprints, or playing with a stick and leaving a message. They can be sunny, happy places full of children's laughter and fun, or wild and lonely strands, heavy with a melancholy grey charm.

Well, I love walking on the beach. But they can be strange, foreboding landscapes, peopled by fairies and pixies of the folklore of the sea...

It was a blustery day in October. I was walking alone on a remote beach in the wilds of Norfolk. Heavy clouds sat gloomily in the lowering sky, threatening squally rain. I pulled...

"Excuse me! When is something going to happen in this pigging story? It's taken you over a hundred and forty words just to get here!"

This sudden outburst shook me from my reveries, and…

"Hoi! Cloth ears, did you hear me?"

I looked around me in surprise. There was no-one in sight. There was just…

"Yeah, yeah, I know, the cry of the gulls wheeling overhead, blah, blah, blah."

Still at a loss to know where this voice had come from, I scanned the beach from horizon to shore but saw no-one. Could this place be haunted by the ghost of some long-dead mariner, I wondered, shipwrecked in a gale on a stormy…?

"You're not going to do that crappy old *seafarer's spirit* routine are you? Oh, come on, be a bit more original than that!"

The voice was soft but not subtle. What's the word? Irritating. Yes, that was it, irritating.

I felt compelled to reply.

"I find stories that contain phantoms quite fun, actually."

I delivered this in a hurt tone, but had no idea to whom I was speaking. If anyone.

"Fine, if that's where you like to be as a writer. But you should try and be a little more daring, pop out of your comfort zone a bit. Vary things, spice it up. Make it readable. Un-putdownable. Not the usual bilge."

"Un-putdownable? Is that even a word?" I was peeved. Then perplexed. "Anyway, how do you know I'm a writer, mister know-it-all?"

"Well, okay, a page turner then."

There was a short pause, then it changed to a more mocking tone.

"Aspire to be a writer; that would describe you better. It's what you'd like people to think you are, you old fraud." Then, returning to the earlier friendlier intonation, it continued, "Why don't you include a story about me? That would be better."

"What makes you think I'd want to include you…" I tailed off, suddenly realising there was absolutely no-one here, that I must be speaking to myself – no, arguing with myself. This was ridiculous!

"Not so fast. No-one there, indeed! Look right down at your feet, dummy. You're not alone, you know."

This last phrase sounded not a little sinister, and I don't mind admitting I was spooked.

"Left foot. You'll need to dig a little."

This made me step back. Where my left foot had been there was something showing through the sand. Something that glinted, even though the light was not bright.

"Careful, be careful. It's a bit fragile now."

I scraped at the sand, taking care as instructed, and soon saw what looked at first like a frosted piece of glass; but as I dug further it revealed a bottle. A whole bottle. With a final pull it came free from its muddy prison, and I wiped it as much as I could.

The glass had become misty, ground from its transparency, I assumed by rolling back and forth in the waves. I could just make out a small figure wedged inside: some sort of carving, I guessed. There was that voice again – I nearly dropped the thing. It spoke!

"Well, that's a bit better. At least I can see it's light outside now."

I turned it over to get a better view, holding it up to the light.

"Hey, don't shake me about! I've had enough of all that, rolling backwards and forwards in those blessed waves!"

I fumbled, wanting to ask it any number of the many questions that now flooded my brain, but I was suddenly struck almost speechless.

"What, I mean what… Well what exactly, I mean, are you?" I at last articulated this staccato piece of verbalisation.

"Good question. I'm a sort of jinn. I think that's what I'm called in your bit of world."

The little thing in this bottle in front of me was now speaking very clearly. A genie! This was surreal, but in a way exciting. He, well I assumed it was a he, gave a big sigh.

"Now you're going to ask how many sodding wishes I can grant you. They always do."

I confess the old legends and stories had been running through my mind, and not least among my thoughts was the wishes thing. My powers of speech came tumbling back.

"Well, I have a lot of other things puzzling me: answers I'd like to know. Things like, have I bumped my head and you're the result of concussion? Am I dreaming this? Are you just a figment of my over-active imagination? Oh yes, and how many wishes?"

"Aha, I thought so. Now, get me out of here and we can discuss things properly."

Advancing to the nearby waves, I carefully washed the remaining sediment from the bottle and then began to struggle with what looked like a cork, or some sort of bung. No joy.

"What's keeping you?" The little guy was getting tetchy. I didn't want to smash the bottle. Or did I? No, probably best not, he may get damaged.

"Don't you dare!"

Scary little mind reader. My brain ticked into gear.

"Hang on, if you're some sort of all-powerful being thingy, how come you're stuck in here? I mean, can't you just *alakazoom* your way out or something?"

"*Alakawhat*? Anyway, use your noddle. I'd have done that a couple of hundred years ago if I could; of course I would. But the Great Magician of Threll himself sealed the flask with resin from the sacred Aquoba tree."

"Then how do you think I can open it?"

I was toying with the idea of explosives.

"Use a decent corkscrew, dummy."

I trudged over the shingle bank and back to the car park, carrying this strange cargo. I knew there was a chance I'd find something to do the trick in with all the other junk I kept in the anachronistically named *glove box*, so I rummaged around for a few moments.

I soon found a scratched pair of sunglasses, a grubby cloth, a biro with no ink, and a charging cable. No corkscrew though. Then I had the clichéd light bulb moment. I went to the boot and found a bent screwdriver.

"Be careful – don't break the neck."

I was tempted to ask if he meant his or the bottle, but thought better of it.

"Naughty – you know what I meant."

This mindreading of his was getting tiresome.

"Now..." My tongue protruded as I applied the blade to the blocked-up opening and started to gouge brown gunge out. "Eugh, that smells awful!"

It reminded me of smouldering old socks. I tried to make sure none of it fell in the car.

"Slowly, slowly."

There was the sound of gasping noises, followed by deep breaths, the kind you take when you first get to the seaside.

"Ahh! Wonderful!"

With a final *plop* the last bit of seal came out. And then, just as suddenly, out popped the tiny spirit fellow, bouncing on to the tarmac.

"Not an elegant entrance, but hey. Thanks mate!"

He stood up, brushing himself down, coughed, and looked around. He looked to be about four inches tall, with pinkish skin, wearing a green silken cloak and striped red and white breeches. His little turned-up shoes were silver and pointy, and he had a bright yellow hat.

"Don't you dare say I look cute or you're for it!"

I don't think cute was on my list of what to say next. Well, maybe I'd thought it for a moment.

He began dancing some sort of jig, which looked comical without any music. Struck by another thought, I felt in my coat pocket and pulled out the little camera I always carry on my walks. I thought I'd get a quick snap – let alone other people believing me, I wanted to believe it all myself.

"No, no photos," he shouted, screwing up his face and holding up a tiny hand.

"I wish you'd keep still, so I can…"

I was interrupted by a bright orange flash. There was an odd aroma, like old cooking oil. I looked down at the ground.

Where the little genie had been there was now a beautiful little figurine. It was about four inches tall, with pinkish skin, and wore a green silken cloak and striped red and white breeches. The little turned-up shoes were silver and pointy, and he had a bright yellow hat. I picked it up, and saw that the face wore a sad, forlorn look.

So, my question was answered. Just the one wish then.

18 JOURNEY TO A NEW LIFE

Gwen Bunting

The ship was running out of fresh water, someone had not tightened the tap on the barrel when they filled their mugs, leaving it dribbling overnight, The biting cold wind froze the water, making the deck slippery.

The lookout shouted, 'icebergs ahead!'

They needed to steer clear of these dangerous masses of ice, nine tenths of them being under the water line. These large loose, floating blocks breaking up into smaller sections would make good drinking water after it was boiled. The crew and the able bodied men would attempt to fish out the smaller lumps of ice to melt them for drinking water.

Barbara Davidson had married Thomas Carmichael in the spring of 1888 and had one baby already, with another on the way. Their life on the Isle of Skye was very hard and the land was not easy to farm, so they had decided to emigrate to Nova Scotia in the hope that it would improve their lives.

Thomas was a baker. He had tried to run his own bakery on Skye but many of the crofters would bake their own bread; it was a way of life. So he decided a new life in another country would be better.

Neither Barbara nor Thomas were good sailors. Barbara having morning sickness did not help. Their year-old son, Dougal, was a handful. He played with the other children and it was noisy down in the hold, but far too dangerous up on deck as the boat tossed in the rough seas.

They were told the journey would take twenty to forty days depending on the weather. Today was day thirty. They seemed to have made good time; the captain on his nightly addressing of the passengers was pleased with their progress.

They passed huge floating icebergs, with colonies of seals riding the waves. The sea was teeming with fish, so crew and passengers were well fed. Many of the men enjoyed passing time by hanging a rod over the side of the boat but only when the sea was calmer.

The cattle in the hold would be fresh stock to farm in the new life in Nova Scotia. They were very noisy and did not stop during the night, disturbing everyone. It was a wonder none of them fell over when the boat rocked from port to starboard, but the presumption was that, being so tightly packed, they held each other up. They would find out when eventually they landed and disembarked.

Barbara wondered if she had made the right decision to emigrate, but really she had no say in the matter. Men in the 1800's never considered their wives opinions; they just did what they wanted to do. Barbara had gone along with it as usual. She hoped that if they were successful in Nova Scotia perhaps her brothers would take the initiative and follow them.

She was woken by severe pains in her stomach and got up to relieve herself, only to find she was miscarrying the baby. She made it to the latrines where, fortunately, there was another woman who immediately gave help.

Nearby they found a room that held a pile of canvas sail. Barbara lay down, writhing in agony.

With help from the other woman the stillborn child was born. and Barbara was conscious enough to understand that the woman was telling her it was a girl.

Barbara lost consciousness and finally stopped breathing, the blood loss bringing a swift end to the young woman's life.

Now the woman must find the dead woman's husband, she did not even know his name.

Suddenly, the boat lurched to starboard. Screams filled the air. The woman carefully wrapped Barbara and her stillborn child in some of the sailcloth and tried to hold on to her, but the churning of the ocean was too strong and she lost her grip. Barbara and her child were swept into the sea and lost out of sight.

Everyone on board was trying to get into the lifeboats, the first-class passengers attempting to take suitcases with them. These were thrown overboard to make room for the women and children.

From the lifeboats they could see in the distance a lighthouse beacon flashing. Those who could row pulled heavily on the oars trying to make for the light and, hopefully, the coastline.

Thomas had managed to get into a boat because he had Dougal in his arms, otherwise he would have been left on the sinking boat. He was frantically looking for Barbara in any of the boats near him.

As dawn was breaking, they could see clearly the lighthouse in the distance. They rowed hard and finally neared the coast, the locals bringing their own boats out to help.

The whole village was waiting on the beach to offer warm clothing and food, taking some into their homes where a fire would be burning bright and warming their chilled bodies.

Still clinging onto Dougal, Thomas was panic-stricken as he could find no trace of Barbara. He was calling her name when a woman approached him, the woman who had helped Barbara.

She asked him questions about Barbara what she was wearing and told him of her sad experience and that her body and the baby were lost to the sea.

He screamed out with rage and ran off hugging Dougal.

The coastline was bleak. He guessed all the helpers came from a fishing village nearby.

Peggy's Cove, the place where the lighthouse stood, was some two hundred miles from their original destination of Halifax, Nova Scotia.

He wondered what life had in store for him and Dougal now.

19 SEA RESCUE

Hilary Woodjets

He was standing on the edge of the harbour wall when I saw him, staring out to sea. It was a chilly day, but the weather was fine, there was hardly a breath of wind and as far as I could tell he was lost in thought.

I suppose I was a bit, too. Jim and I had often walked along this stretch of the beach with our dog Marshall. When we were a lot younger, Jim sometimes turned cartwheels on the sand, and we would run into the sea together, laughing and squealing as the coldness of the sea hit us. Bathing in the north North Sea is not for the faint-hearted. It might kill you. Seriously.

The compatibility of dodgy tickers with sudden extremes of temperatures is not well-known, chiefly because it isn't. Which is why nowadays, it is only my toes that go for a dip and only those when the weather is more than 20°. None of those with beach bodies honed to perfection want to see an old lady in her cozzie turning purple. It's bad enough that my toes do.

Anyway, after Jim had stopped turning cartwheels, and the only wheels that turned were those on his wheelchair, he sank slowly into an advanced form of some kind of premature old age decrepitude. We would often come out here just to let Marshall have a good run along the beach, chasing his other doggy pals and having a high old time.

Of course, we would have to walk out along the wall as it became impossible to wheel Jim's chair in the sand. So we would walk along the hard surface of the little harbour, stand and admire the boats, and then go to look at the sea when it was in a tranquil mood.

While he still had the power of lucid speech, he would wax lyrical about the beauty of the sunrises and the cloudscapes, the foaming 'white horses' of the waves, and the raucous cries of the seagulls as they hovered and dipped with the wind. Latterly he would just sit and gaze at the surface of the sea. He was unable to lift his head to see the glories of the sky scapes, the surrounding dunes covered in sea grasses, the children building sandcastles and searching for shells or sea-glass.

Then Marshall did what all animals do: he died and left a gaping hole in our hearts. We had him cremated. Jim had already told me a long time ago that he wanted our boy's ashes scattered with his own from the sea wall.

When Jim died just a matter of three weeks later, not only did I feel that the hole in my heart got bigger, I began to understand why doctors now say there is such a thing as 'broken heart syndrome'.

We'd had no children and our parents were long gone. Although Jim had a brother living in Devon and a sister living in Inverness, we – living more or less equidistantly between – had been the ones to travel to one end of the country or the other, to make the phone calls, to keep in touch. They hadn't bothered coming to the funeral, claiming distance and old age, leaving me with my thoughts and a couple of tubes of ashes, one for Marshall and one for Jim.

So, when I saw this man, almost militarily erect, with a tube under his arm, I knew exactly what he was doing. He wet his finger, stuck it up in the air, and then, deciding there wasn't enough wind to blow the remains back over him, he took the tube from under his arm, opened the lid, knelt down and poured the ashes into the sea, where they leapt and frolicked with the waves gently beating against the wall.

As I had been about to perform the same task, I waited for a few minutes to see whether he would be leaving. It didn't seem very respectful of me to immediately embark on emptying the ashes in my possession while he was still in the vicinity, so I sat on the bench not too far away from him, put the bag that held the tubes next to me, and waited.

Suddenly, I heard his howl of anguish, and saw that he was climbing the railings over the harbour wall!

'Hey!' I cried. 'What are you doing?'

By this time I had run to grab his coat sleeve, but he was having none of it.

'Get off me, you stupid woman! I want to let go!'

'But you mustn't do it like this! You must have friends and people who love you. Please don't jump!'

I was hanging on to him for fear of the grim death he might be letting himself in for. Although, truth to tell, he was more likely to dash his brains out on the rocks that weren't that far below.

By this time, we had caused a bit of a commotion, so another man had come to help me restrain him and get him back over the railings.

'Come on, old fella, nothing's that bad. Come on and let's get you a nice warm cup of tea.'

Having got him stood between us, he shook us off angrily, swore and said 'I don't *want* a bloody cup of tea! I want my car keys! Look - there they are on the rocks down there, and I was trying to get down to get them!'

All three of us leaned on the railings and peered down to the rocks below, just in time to see a wave lift them effortlessly off one of the flatter rocks and carry them off with the receding tide.

The man let his head slump forward onto his chest. I could see him balling his fists, and I took a step backwards as he turned to me, brown eyes blazing, his face red with anger.

'You stupid, interfering... arrgh... RIDICULOUS woman!'

His voice rose with every epithet.

'Oi! There's no need for that!' The man who had helped me get him back over the railings said.

'I'm so sorry; I thought you were trying to commit suicide, and I didn't want to stand by and just watch you do it. That's why I thought I was trying to help you.'

I could feel tears starting to form in my eyes, and I really didn't want to cry in front of this unpleasant man. 'I can only apologise.'

'No, you can do more than that. I have a car but no keys to start it with. I need to get home to get my other set. Perhaps you would be good enough to drive me there and then bring me back so that I can pick up my car.'

His voice dripped with so much venom that I very nearly said 'no'.

But then, I thought since it was my fault that he didn't get to attain his objective of collecting his keys from their watery grave, I sighed, said yes, I'd do that, and walked back towards my car, picking up Marshall and Jim on the way.

'Would you like to get in?' I unlocked the car and put Marshall and Jim in the boot. (Marshall had been used to it, with his exuberant entrance into the main body of the saloon stopped by a wire mesh cage. Poor Jim would never have got in the boot when he was alive, I thought to myself with a smile.).

'Not really', said the man. 'When did you last clean out the interior? And it smells of dog!'

At this point, my temper flared.

'Do you want a lift home or not? It smells of dog because it's the last reminder I have of a faithful companion. And I lost my wonderful husband as well not long after and both quite recently. So get in, you horrid man, sit down, tell me your address and then SHUT UP!'

We drove to his home in stony silence. His house was in what Jim and I used to call 'Millionaire's Row', although many of the houses, which had probably had servants to maintain the houses and gardens when built in the late 19th Century, had now been divided into flats. A few hadn't, though, and his was one such. A beautiful wisteria graced the front of the house, twisting over the front door and the bay windows. The door was solid oak, none of the cheap plasticky sort here, such as the type that welcomed visitors to our far more humble abode.

Our? I guess I shall have to get used to thinking in terms of 'My'….house, car, garden… and all the jobs that Jim used to do, like putting out the rubbish bins for collection, arranging insurances, doing tax returns; I didn't want to go down that rabbit-hole just then.

He went into the house, leaving the front door open. I saw a polished wood floor, and a neat and tidy hallway. Unlike ours – mine – where the boots from my last walk with Marshall were still caked in the sand that clung to them, and the smart black court shoes that I wore to Jim's funeral were littered with Jim's old shoes under the hall stand. The man picked up his set of keys, came out of the house and took his seat back in the car.

I turned the key in the ignition.

'Could you stop a moment, please?' he asked.

'I thought you wanted to get back to your car?'

'I do, but before we start off, I think I owe you an apology for my bad behaviour. Can we start again, please?'

He sighed. 'My name is Robert King. The reason I was at the harbour today is because that is where my wife wanted her ashes scattered. She died in a car accident six months ago, and it has taken me until now to face going there. It was one of our favourite places to visit.'

He sat with his head bowed. I thought carefully about what I wanted to say, then thought again before telling him my name and that his apology was accepted.

'I'd gone to the harbour wall on the same errand. My husband died three months ago and it was the first time I had felt able to fulfill the task he wanted, of having his ashes scattered with those of our dog. When I saw you with the tube under your arm, I didn't want to intrude on your grief, but it's also why I thought you were going to commit suicide in your grief. God knows

I have felt like doing that from time to time. Sometimes it just gets to be a bit much… you know?'

He reached across and took my hand. 'Yes, I do.'

A minute or so passed in silence between us, and then I thought we had perhaps better get going. So, I turned the key again, and we set off on the journey back towards the harbour.

I parked my car next to his pristine Lexus, hoping some of the shine might rub off onto mine, and got ready to see him off.

But he didn't go.

'My wife and I used to have a cup of coffee and a scone in the café over there after we'd had our walk along the harbour wall. Why don't you take Jim and Marshall and scatter their ashes, then perhaps we can go for a cuppa afterwards - if you want to, that is? Take as long as you like, I can wait. I'm in no rush.'

'Do you mind if I see how I feel when I get back?'

'Of course not.'

He smiled, and I could see that he had kind eyes, and the sort of wrinkles a face gets when it normally laughs a lot. 'But I hope you will, so that I can make some sort of amends.'

I retrieved Jim and Marshall from the boot of the car and walked slowly towards the end of the harbour wall. It's a very final thing to get rid of the last remains of those you have loved and lost. Whether it's their ashes, or letters from a former boy- or girlfriend, or the last bits of grandma's china.

….And there I was, scattering the ashes of my old dog, who sat with me as I cried through Jim's worst days of illness, and those of my husband, my soul mate, my other – and some would say, better – half.

I watched as they fell into the sea and washed against the wall. I cried silently as I packed the tubes back in the plastic carrier bag I'd brought them in, and then I sat for a while on the bench.

The sea is never the same two days running - or even two hours running. It changes its character as it ebbs and flows with the tides. It can be your solace in its tranquility and match your anger and be terrifyingly frightening in its wrath. It can be the memory of happy times, and the wonder of quiet reflective ones.

'But it never, ever stands still and stagnates.'

I sat bolt upright. I'm not one for believing in ghosts, but I heard Jim's voice as clear as day intrude on those thoughts. I even looked around to see whether he was there, although I knew that couldn't be possible.

I hadn't realised that the wind was beginning to get up and I had become quite chilled, so I gathered up the bag with its tubes, silently waved a last goodbye to the two most wonderful souls I had known, and went back to the cars, forty-five minutes after I had left.

Robert got out to greet me. 'How do you feel?'

'Cold', I smiled.

'Then shall we go and get that cup of coffee?'

And that, dear friends, is how you come to be celebrating our marriage with us, now five years down the line from that first, seemingly disastrous meeting.

Neither of us will ever forget Helen or Jim. Neither of us is taking their places in each other's hearts. We walk alongside them, with both still in our hearts.

But apart from them, Robert and I are ready to make our own story in the autumn of our lives.

20 BED HEAD

Val Chapman

Remember during Covid if you had family over, the police would come and make them go home?

Do you know if that service is still available?

☆☆☆☆☆☆☆☆☆☆☆

I woke up with her foot in my ear.

Not for the first time it has to be said.

Our daughter and her husband were on a "child-free" holiday and we had the dubious honour of looking after their two children.

I have some recollections of bringing up our three back in the "good old days", and it was a bit of a steep learning curve at the time. Which is true in the same way that Everest is "a bit hilly".

But this?

This seemed much tougher somehow. I put it down to an age thing. Ours as well as theirs.

Daytimes had been, by and large, fine. As they lived at the seaside, we spent plenty of time building sandcastles, collecting shells and exploring rock pools. They might not have wanted to go quite as often, preferring to stay home to watch the latest cartoon on TV, but I was "in my second childhood" and loving it.

There were some tricky moments to deal with, I'm not going to lie.

Between them they had "issues" such as...

The milk was "too loud."

I wouldn't let her eat a battery, or stick her finger in some dog poo.

I refused to take the bones out of his leg.

He insisted on knowing how mermaids had babies.

She wants her socks off, because they smell funny and don't taste nice. (I'm not sure these aren't connected.)

Anyway, despite these "quirks" we had plenty of fun in the park, at the beach or playing with the mountain of toys they have.

The main bone of contention was sleep.

Neither of them seem to have got the hang of it, and all the sea air we exposed them to, hoping to tire them out, had no effect. Luckily, there were two of us to deal with the two of them.

This particular night, darling granddaughter was proving the trickiest. Wanting to show how it was done, I elected to sort it out. Deciding that keeping her in our bed wasn't an option, I took her back to her room, trying to keep calm when I stood on a dead crab she had brought back from our day out.

Quickly realising that she wasn't going to settle any time soon I climbed into bed with her, and we snuggled down.

All was fine for a couple of hours, until the aforementioned foot in my ear.

I looked across at the sleeping starfish, thankfully seeing her still fast asleep. I lay there for a few minutes, wondering to myself if I could risk going back to our bed without waking the little angel. The decision was taken out of my hands however as, being of a certain age, I needed to go to the toilet.

As you are all probably aware, there are nights when you just know you won't be able to get back to sleep, and this appeared to be one of those times.

A cup of tea might help.

I made my way downstairs to the kitchen.

I had just made my cuppa and was carrying it to the table when in the semi darkness I stubbed my toe on the chair leg.

I'll admit I swore a bit, then sat down and tried to rub the pain away.

It was then I noticed a small pool of liquid, possibly water, underneath the wine cooler.

Yes, they have a wine cooler. Don't ask.

Great, I have no idea what that could be.

It may have been the pain, the frustration, the exhaustion, or all three, but I put my head in my hands and just sobbed.

I hadn't noticed my grandson come into the kitchen.

He put his little arms around me and whispered, "Why are you crying? Is it because of your hair?"

Thanks sweetheart, so, now I have four things to cry about...

21 THE SHELL COLLECTOR

Phil Cumberland

"How long have you been a collector of seashells, Mr Gault?"

Detective Inspector Sands of Norfolk Constabulary was standing on the beach near Hemsby. On a late evening in late May, he was talking to a man in his late fifties.

"I can't remember exactly, Inspector. I did it a bit as a boy; part time since then. Since partially retiring, I do it mainly evenings in the summer and at the weekends. Not every weekend, and not every evening. Usually, after the tide has gone out leaving the flotsam below the tide line."

"Do you normally visit this particular part of the shoreline?"

"Not often, no. About once a fortnight on average. The cove is small with high sand cliffs and if you misjudge the incoming tide you have to swim for it – that's if you have the time."

"Can you go through the events of this evening please?"

"I finished work at four pm, walked home, had a meal with my wife. Sometimes she comes with me and the dog comes too but she wasn't up to a lot and stayed at home with Rufus, our dog. Sunset isn't until about ten pm. I left our house at around seven and was in the cove by about seven thirty. There was a fair bit of flotsam laying about, a lot of whelk and cockle shells. I collected up the better ones and put them in my bucket. I have that large yellow plastic bucket you can see to put the shells in, and I wash them off when I get home. About once a week I take my finds to the shell shop in town and they buy any they like off me. I had found this really large shell and was pleased about it then when I noticed something white in the sand. I nearly ignored it, for a start it looked like a large white stone or rock, but when I looked again I noticed that it didn't look quite right for a stone. I walked over and dug around near it with my trowel when I saw the eye sockets and the other hole, I phoned the police."

"And you hadn't noticed these remains before?"

"No, it was on part of the beach I don't often visit, behind the big rocks. Most of the shells wash up in front of them. I had noticed a particularly large winkle shell, a large spiral shell. It was when I went to pick that up I saw what turned out to be the skull."

"Why do you think it wasn't visible before?"

"Probably the action of the tides, the rocks would have broken the force of the waves but sometimes the tides can scour more than at other times."

"I see, is there anything else you can think of that might be useful for our enquiry."

As there was nothing else he thought he would tell DI Sands, Gault thoughtfully set off for home.

His wife had been shocked to hear of his discovery. He had phoned her after calling the police to let her know he might be later than usual before he returned home. By the time he arrived home his wife had gone to bed.

The dawn had brought with it a thought or two. After dressing and breakfast, John Gault's trawl of the internet provided some results.

He couldn't remember the date, only a report of a couple missing from a morning walk. Eventually the archives of the Eastern Daily Press of eight years earlier yielded some details under a headline of Holiday Couple Reported Missing.

A young couple had left their boarding house for an early morning walk but failed to return on that or the following day. A search failed to find any trace of them. A few days later, however, the husband's body washed ashore further up the coast. Of the wife there was no sign. There was no mention of the cliff collapse at the time, in the cove where the skeleton was found.

He was seldom home in those days, working away often. When he returned and visited the cove for a shell hunt the fall of sand from the cliff had been deposited on the beach. By that time, the husband's body had been found and the assumption made was the couple had been washed away by the sea. The wife's body had never been found.

He had once considered the likelihood that the cliff fall might have been significant in covering the body. John decided to share these thoughts with the inspector and pulled Sands' card from his pocket. He hesitated, deciding to talk to his wife first about the earlier incident. She worked at the village shop and might remember details he had forgotten.

John's wife Gwen was a later riser than he, and he took an eight o'clock cup of tea to help her see in the day. When he saw that Gwen was fully conscious and sipping from the mug he shared his thoughts with her.

"That skeleton I found yesterday at the beach under the cliffs... do you remember that couple who disappeared about eight years ago, Mr and Mrs Moore? The husband's body washed up a few days later but his wife's was never found."

"Vaguely. They had been in the shop a few times while they were here on holiday. They were a nice couple from what I can remember. We put a poster up in the shop. There was a photo in their room at the boarding house, and the police used that."

"Can you remember anything else, Gwen?"

"It's eight years ago, John, I have a job remembering what I was doing yesterday, let alone eight years ago."

John went downstairs, sat in front of his laptop with the Eastern Daily Press archives on the screen, and called D I Sands on his mobile phone. The call was soon answered.

"D I Sands?"

"Yes, who's calling?"

"It's John Gault. We met last night on the beach, I discovered the body."

"How can I help you, Mr Gault?"

"I should have said this last night... While you are investigating the remains in the cove, please make sure your team are aware of the tide movement. There is a proper safe fallback plan in place, if the tide catches them out. Oh, and was it a complete skeleton you found? I noticed the hole in the front of the skull."

"Thank you for your suggestion Mr Gault, I will pass it on. Yes, it appears that it may be a complete or near complete skeleton and no we have no idea as to its identity, but we think from remains of clothing it may be female."

"While I was walking home, I vaguely remembered a couple who went missing a few years ago. The husband's body washed up a few miles away, but his wife was never found. It was assumed she had drowned, and her body was lost to the sea.

"I looked on the internet and found information on the Eastern Daily Press website. The couple's name was Moore and they disappeared in May 2016. About that time, I think there was a cliff fall which may have covered the body with sand. In the years following, the tides could have washed away the sand to uncover the skeleton."

"Thank you, Mr Gault. It's before my time but I'm sure some of my colleagues will remember it."

Sands ended the call and swung around on his chair to face his team in the incident room'

"Where are we with the post mortem, Judy?"

"I'll phone the pathologist, guv."

Detective Sergeant Judith Wiles, was Sands' second in command, a responsible capable, woman in her early forties. Five minutes later, she walked over to Sands' desk and told him the post mortem was at three pm that afternoon.

The phone rang in the incident room. DS Wiles answered it.

She put a hand over the mouthpiece, turned to the room and announced, "They've found another skeleton."

Sands, replied, "Where?"

"Near to the first one apparently. They were digging around trying to find a murder weapon when they found it."

"So there are two bodies there now, is that correct?"

"That seems to be the case; there are no other details so far."

D. I. Sands arrived at the mortuary promptly at three and was shown into the pathologist's examination room. Like many police officers, it wasn't his favourite place.

"What have we got Doc?"

The pathologist, Doctor Strang, was portly and bald. He was, Sands guessed, sixtyish in age.

Strang looked up from the corpse he had been examining.

"The deceased was female, in her thirties I would guess. She doesn't appear to have given birth to any children. The cause of death is, I would say, a bullet wound to the head, Given the position of the entry and exit wounds, I would say the shot came from above. Death would have been instantaneous."

"Are there any other injuries?"

"Only a broken left femur, an old injury that had healed. The victim didn't appear to be fully clothed. There was no underwear apparent, just a sundress sitting around her waist. I have sent out a search with the dental records for an ID."

"It looks like you are in for a busy time of it Doc. They've found another body."

"Yes, I have heard and will be making my way there very shortly."

"As will I."

When Sands arrived at the cove, a barrier of sandbags had been erected to, hopefully, stop the tide encroaching on the crime scene.

An inflatable dinghy sitting on the sand was tied up to the sandbags, and a long ladder had been fixed to what was hoped to be a safe part of the cliff. The doctor had been and gone, having had no problem declaring life extinct. The second skeletal remains showed that it, too, had suffered a head wound. There was no clothing on the body.

Sands and Strang stood together looking at the recently unearthed corpse. The forensics team were searching the scene away from this and the site of the body found earlier.

"What do you think, Doc?"

"It's a similar wound; my guess is they were both shot from above with a high-powered rifle."

"Fortuitous that the cliff collapsed when it did, covering the bodies."

"Very, if you were the perpetrator."

"Do you think it's possible that the cliff fall was deliberately staged by the shooter to cover the bodies?"

"Given the position of the wounds, I would think it has to be a distinct possibility."

At that moment there was a shout from one of the search team, a young woman in white overalls and masked. Sands wondered given the passage of time and the location whether that was strictly necessary.

"Sir, we have found a pair of trousers, a mobile phone and a camera in its case. The mobile phone isn't in very good condition, but the camera case could be waterproof."

"Is there anything in the pockets?"

"A wallet, and there is a driving licence inside."

"Who does it belong to?"

The young woman walked over to join Sands and the pathologist. She pulled out the driving licence and showed it to Sands.

"I see... a Mr Ralph Smith. Are those business cards, miss?"

"Underwood, Sylvia. Yes, they are. A bit damp, but Mr Smith seems to have been a photographer. Shall I bag up the camera sir?"

Sands pulled out his phone to photograph the driving licence and business card while Sylvia held them.

"Yes please, when you can. Would it be possible to see if there is anything on the camera we can look at? I know it's an old murder, but I would like to put it to bed as soon as I can."

"We'll do our best."

"Thank you, Sylvia. I would appreciate it. Oh, can you see if there is another phone anywhere? I would think they both would have had one."

In the meantime, Sands and Strang had been joined by DS Judy Wiles.

"I haven't brought my bucket and spade, guv."

"You won't need them; there are plenty lying about here already."

"The tide is coming in. We'd better get to higher ground."

Sands informed the team. Sandbags which had been removed to allow passage to the crime scene were quickly replaced, and everyone headed off around the end of the cove, to the higher, safer ground of the main beach and promenade. A constable remained on the beach to guard the crime scene, as close to its taped off perimeter as was safe.

DI Sands called his small team together for the briefing early next day.

"We have the remains of two bodies, one male and one female, almost certainly murder victims. Each was killed by a single round from a high powered rifle shot to the head. We believe that the male body is that of Mr Ralph Smith, a photographer. The other – the female – could be that of Mrs Susan Moore. The body of her husband, Mr William Moore, was washed up ashore a few days after they were reported missing.

"We have also found what we believe to be Smith's camera and a mobile phone. Smith's wallet was in the pocket of what we believe to be his trousers. He wasn't wearing them when he was killed apparently."

DS Wiles raised her hand.

"Yes, Judy."

"Are we thinking Mr Moore killed his wife and the photographer, then started the cliff fall, fell down with it and got washed away by the incoming tide?"

"That's a possibility, but where is the gun?"

"Washed away by the tide or still buried in the sand?"

"It's possible. Can you try and trace the next of kin for Mrs Moore and Mr Smith. . If so, by whom? Take DC Roberts with you and pop round to see Mr Gault first, update him about the other body and ask him what he knows about Smith."

DS Wiles and DC Roberts set off leaving a thoughtful Sands sitting behind a desk in the incident room.

Mr Gault was at work when Wiles and Roberts called. Mrs Gault asked them if she could help.

Maybe DS Wiles shouldn't have mentioned finding a second body, as Mrs Gault went white with shock and had to sit down. She did say her husband would be home at about four-thirty pm. DS Wiles said they would return after Mr Gault was expected home.

"Why do you think the news of the second body shook Mrs Gault up?" asked DC Roberts.

"I don't know, Jim."

Ralph Smith's home address – the one on his driving licence – was in the nearby inland village of Ingsby.

The knock on the door of the tidy, detached bungalow was answered by a fair-haired woman, in her forties, Judy would have guessed; Mrs Smith, it transpired. Once they had identified themselves, they were invited into the bungalow and shown into the lounge.

As soon as they were seated, Mrs Smith said, "This is about Ralph isn't it? I haven't seen him for about eight years."

Judy answered, "I'm sorry to inform you but we have found a body we think may be that of your husband, Mrs Smith."

"Where did you find him?"

"Along the coast in Scremby. We are treating the death as suspicious."

"I wish I could say I was surprised or sorry. He was a nasty bit of work. He always had a problem keeping it in his trousers. Last I heard he had rented a Chalet in Scremby and was doing freelance photography, probably photographing married women without their clothes on."

"I see. Didn't you think it odd when he didn't contact you?"

"No. I thought, good riddance. He had probably got himself shacked up with a woman somewhere, and I was glad he was gone."

Mrs Smith hadn't anything of her husband's they could sample for DNA. She said she had thrown out everything of his years ago.

As they hadn't any contact details for Mrs Moore's next of kin, they returned to the station.

The post-mortem for skeleton number two was scheduled for three pm that afternoon. Judy Wiles updated Sands about the results of their enquiries.

"Can you try to find out where this chalet is that Smith rented, Judy, and did he own a car?"

"I'm sorry, I didn't think to ask."

"OK, these things happen. Jim can you make enquiries? Phone Mrs Smith first, then check on the DVLA database."

Sands was surprised when he had a call from forensics. Although the battery in the camera wasn't in good condition, the rest of the contents of the camera bag were – in particular, the memory card inside the camera and some others stored in the bag.

"Change of plan, Jim. Nip into Norwich and go to the forensics lab. They will copy all the files from the camera's cards onto a USB stick. Can you get it back here ASAP? I want to see who he was taking pictures of."

Judy Wiles contacted the two companies that rented out holiday chalets in Scremby. She drew a blank with the first company but was luckier with Happy Holidays Holiday Chalets.

The owner vaguely remembered the name, Ralph Smith. She said she would check the records and get back in touch when she had the information. While she was waiting, Judy phoned Mrs Smith and asked if her husband owned a car. He didn't, or hadn't at the time he disappeared.

"When he needed one, he rented one. He used a bike or a bus mostly; he said he could see more from a bus or on his bike."

Jim Roberts arrived back from Norwich at two thirty with the memory stick containing the copied files from Smith's camera and the other memory cards in the camera case. Sands asked them to look through the photos and note anything that might be useful.

He set off for the mortuary and the post mortem.

Strang gave the cause of death as a gunshot wound to the head, with death likely to have been instantaneous. He couldn't definitely say whether the two deceased victims were killed with the same weapon as the bullets had yet to be recovered but thought it highly likely.

Sands returned to the station, reflecting on the probable sequence of events, the identity of the killer and a possible motive. The most likely suspect was William Moore, but no weapon had been found. His post mortem indicated nothing but drowning as a cause of death. It is possible he could have hit his head as the cliff collapsed, and he fell as a result.

Sands would send for the original post mortem.

When he walked into the incident room Judy Wickes called him over.

"You might want to see this Guv."

Sands went to look at the screen of her computer. Two naked women were engaged in sexual activity with each other. One appeared to be Susan Moore; the other was unknown to Sands.

"I see. One of these ladies appears to be Susan Moore. The other one I don't recognise."

"The other woman appears to be Mrs Gault, who Jim and I met this morning."

Jim Roberts walked over at the mention of his name,

"Yes, that's Mrs Gault. Crikey, what on earth is that in her hand? Is that going where I think it is?"

Judy moved the cursor and the next picture in the sequence appeared.

"Yes, it seems it did."

A few pictures further on, it seemed that Ralph Smith was enjoying Mrs Gault's hospitality. And, further on, Mrs Moore's.

"Ten out of ten for stamina," remarked Judy.

Sands asked, "On a more practical note, do we know when these photos were taken?"

"Just before Mr Moore's body was discovered. About a week earlier."

"Thank you, Judy. Are there any other photos on these cards that are relevant to the enquiry?"

"I don't think so but will keep checking. Most of the rest are totally innocent: sea views and portraits, some wedding photos."

"Are there any photos of the cliff top, the part where it collapsed? It would be interesting if there were any visible cracks or fault?"

"I will have a look through the pictures."

Jim Roberts called out, 'We've just had a call from the manager of the company that rented out the chalet to Ralph Smith.

"He disappeared overnight. The chalet was emptied of his possessions. They discovered he had gone early one morning; the door had been left open and they didn't get the key back."

DI Sands called his team together.

"Right, we need to have a word with Mrs Gault to find out more about her relationship with Mrs Moore and Mr Smith."

Just then, the phone rang. DC Roberts answered it. After a few moments, he called out to Sands.

"Guv, I think you need to take this. It's Mrs Gault."

Sands picked up his phone as Roberts transferred the call to him.

"Good afternoon, Mrs Gault. How can I help you?"

Her voice was distraught.

"I know who killed Sue and Ralph. Meet me at my husband's allotment. Now, before he gets home."

She gave Sands the address, Sands, Wiles and Roberts set off to meet her.

It was a large shed for an allotment. The door had been forced open; a large crowbar lay on the ground by the open door.

Mrs Gault in blue jeans and a white sweatshirt stood by the open door. Her face was wet with tears.

"I haven't touched anything apart from opening the other door and the cupboard inside. I hadn't noticed the other door before today. I don't come to the allotment often, and if I hadn't been in such a temper I wouldn't have knocked over the racking in front of it."

The shed had been partitioned. The dividing wall was as sturdy as the rest of the windowless building.

The door had put up a fight, but it too stood open. Inside, a steel cupboard had been opened. Its door had been forced, and on the shelves were a printer and photographic equipment. In a corner of this room within the shed stood a bicycle. There were also two suitcases sitting on the floor. A tall secure steel cupboard secured to the shed wall was untouched.

Mrs Gault continued, "This is Ralph's stuff. I didn't know it was here. I didn't know about this other room.

"Susan, Ralph and I were going to move in together. John must have found out and then killed Ralph and Susan. I thought they had just left without me to start a new life together. When I visited the chalet and found it empty, that confirmed it for me."

"We found some intimate photographs in Mr Smith's camera", Said Sands.

"Ralph was going to sell them to a magazine owner he knew, to help finance our move. I loved them both. Why did they have to die?"

With that she burst into tears. Judy instinctively rushed over to put her arms around her and tried to comfort her.

Two uniformed constables started to mark off the cordon while the forensics team began checking, bagging and logging the shed's contents.

The steel cupboard contained a high-powered rifle with a telescopic sight and a shotgun bag, no doubt used to carry the rifle without arousing suspicion. The two hand grenades in the cupboard weren't too much of a surprise. Possibly a grenade had caused the cliff fall.

The discovery that Gault had been a long-serving army sergeant, finishing his career in ordnance supplies before retiring, was certainly considered significant.

He was arrested as he returned home from work.

22 MUDDY WATERS

Cathy Cade

Faye had never seen the attraction of mud-whomping, but her kids loved to wallow in the coastal estuary mud. Now, the tide was coming in fast, so Adam and his friend had abandoned the mud, bringing their bucket up from the saltings to the standpipe.

Adam tipped out salt water.

"No, don't do that."

Too late; he'd topped up the bucket with tap water. Now the cockles would have to be cooked.

"They'd have kept longer in salt water."

Adam scowled. "I know what I'm doing. They have to breathe clean water to flush out the grit."

Jake smirked. "He's been on a wilderness course, innit? Like that programme on telly."

Adam retrieved cockles that had escaped with the water. "I already knew how to sail and stuff. I dunno why you sent me on that Survival Summer Camp anyway."

To enjoy two weeks of peace, thought Faye, without you and Amy fighting like rats in a bucket.

Before he went to the camp, Adam had asked if he could bring his friend to the caravan this summer. Feeling guilty, she had agreed and been relieved when Jake declined the offer.

She wasn't keen on this friend Adam had made since his best friend moved away. Should she say something?

During her own teens, when her mother had spoken out against her sister's boyfriend, her sister had dug her stiletto heels in, rushing into an early, disastrous marriage. Faye believed that, with less opposition her sister would, in time, have figured him out for herself. She wasn't stupid, just stubborn.

Adam could be difficult, but he wasn't stupid. He'd been playing chess with his granddad, for heaven's sake, from the age of six. A summer away from Jake might break the spell.

To her dismay, Jake changed his mind on Adam's return from summer camp. Amy claimed he'd upset someone and wanted to get away from the area while things settled.

Faye comforted herself that at least Jake would keep Adam too busy to torment his sister.

"We don't need to keep the cockles for longer, anyway." Adam moved the bucket into the shade.

"Well, I'm taking Amy shopping," ...*when she's finished deciding what she's going to wear.* "And then we're going to the station to pick up Dad."

Her husband was taking a half day off so that he could join them for bank holiday weekend.

"Then Dad's got to take the gas bottle to the garage. It's nearly empty."

It was the busiest weekend of the summer. All the plot-holders came down for the annual fundraising fete on Sunday, dubbed by Adam, "the fete worse than death".

On Monday they would pack up and drive home for work and school next week. It was the official end of summer. She could hardly wait.

Having this caravan on the estuary where her husband had spent his childhood summers and her children spent theirs, had been a lifesaver when the children were young. But now they were older, they wanted to be with their school friends, and the vacation seemed longer than ever.

The cockles would probably be dead when they got back, fit only for binning.

Jake hadn't shared Adam's enthusiasm for wallowing in mud. His "Why?" when Adam suggested it, had prompted him to justify his suggestion.

Adam had made digging for cockles sound like a cool thing you'd do on a survival course, although the summer camp had only caught fish and scavenged wild plants for campfire meals.

Adam had only recently been accepted by Jake's band of followers and was keen to impress the leader of the pack.

But Jake quickly lost interest in caravan living. There was no wireless internet, and mobile reception was rubbish. The nearest pub was a half-hour walk, and he wasn't impressed by the old bikes that had been retired to the caravan. Adam wouldn't suggest another sailing expedition; Jake had almost capsized the dinghy last time. Maybe when Dad was here…

The sun had moved around the caravan to warm the bucket. "Let's cook the cockles."

How hard could it be?

Adam tipped water onto the grass, but a layer of mud remained at the bottom. He collected the big cooking pot from the shed and transferred cockles in handfuls.

Jake was swearing at his mobile phone, Adam suppressed the disloyal thought that entertaining Jake could be more drudgery than company.

He heaved the pot into the caravan and onto the cooker, where he poured in enough jugs of water to cover the shells. Turning on the big gas ring at the back, he pressed the ignition button. It would take ages for the water to boil.

He was sitting in the sun with Jake and a can of lager when he heard the hiss of the pot boiling over. The steam made it hard to see if the cockles had opened. He pulled the pot towards him, and boiling water slopped over his wrist. His yelp brought Jake to the door.

"Whass up, mate?"

Adam bit back his whimpers and ran the cold tap over the burn, as advised by summer camp first aid. Jake judged it was safe to come in.

"It don't 'arf pong in 'ere."

"Fish, innit." Adam took a steadying breath and turned off the water.

He carefully transferred the pot to the draining board. Jake stood back as he tipped hot water into the sink.

"We've got to throw away any shells that haven't opened." He topped up the pan with jugs of cold water, tipping and topping up until what remained was lukewarm. "We'll have to fish 'em out into smaller bowls."

"The smell's getting worse. I need a fag. Want one?"

"Smoke it outside or they'll smell it when they come back."

"Not over that niff they won't." Jake searched in vain for his matches. Giving up, he resorted to the cooker, turning the knob for a front gas ring. He reached for the ignition button.

"Stop! Don't press it!"

Knobs for the front and back gas rings were presenting at the same angle. "It'll blow up the caravan."

Adam turned off both and spun around to open the nearest window. "The spilled water must have put the flames out."

Jake was already outside.

While Adam opened more windows, Jake found matches under the barbeque. He sat on the caravan steps to light his cigarette and, shaking the match, tossed it over his shoulder.

Fortunately, most of the gas had dispersed, and the damage was mostly cosmetic. But persistent.

Adam was scrubbing when Mum and Amy returned with Dad. The wall looked worse than when he began.

On seeing the blackened kitchen, Jake had stuffed his belongings into his backpack and set off to the station. Dad said they'd passed him on the road, but he didn't wave back. Amy had commented on Jake's blackened hair and the back of his t-shirt as they passed him.

It took superhuman effort to ignore Amy's bursts of giggles as she scrubbed beside him, but Mum was in good spirits despite the mess.

"Looking forward to school next week?"

Amy groaned.

"How about you, Adam?"

He grunted. "Think I'll join the chess club."

23 A SHOREBIRD

Laraine Newsom

Mary was walking her dog along the coast of Cuckmere Haven Beach when Trixie, her Heinz 57 rescue dog of two years, started pulling hard on her leash. She had spotted a bird and wanted to play chase. The bird quickly flew a short distance away. Mary held on tight to Trixie's leash.

The bird appeared tired, Mary wondered if the bird had flown from abroad. She had not seen this type of bird before with its reddish chest, white belly and speckled wings. But what was most distinctive was its long-spoon shaped beak.

Now Trixie was calmer, Mary quickly got out her phone and took a photo.

Mary's husband came home later that evening with the local evening newspaper. She sat down to just flip through the pages. As she did so, a headline caught her eye: "Shorebird seen in East Sussex."

The shorebird was in fact a spoon-billed sandpiper and had come from the Wildfowl and Wetlands Trust in Slimbridge. David had worked at the centre for a number of years and was furious that a window had been left open and the bird had escaped.

The shorebird was part of a captive breeding program to bring the spoon-billed sandpiper back from the brink of extinction. The programme was proving to be successful. David had been so pleased with the success and now felt let down by whoever had been negligent by opening the window. This had happened nearly a week ago.

Mary took a different route when walking her dog next day. She hoped that she would see the shorebird again.

She often walked on the grassy land on higher ground. From this viewpoint she could look across at the Seven Sisters white chalk cliffs. She always marvelled at their beauty and wouldn't want to live anywhere else.

As she drew nearer, she was amazed at the amount of people around, before realising the area was full of twitchers with their large camera lenses and binoculars. She tried to squeeze through the crowd but there was no room for her and her dog to pass.

She walked further away, still hoping for another glimpse of this special bird. She, like David, hoped that the shorebird would keep safe.

She looked up to see the spoon-billed sandpiper take flight. She could have sworn that it was whistling a beautiful melody of freedom.

24 WINEY THE WITCH GOES TO COVEHITHE

Wendy Fletcher

As Winey flew silently through the darkening sky she looked out for familiar landmarks. Beneath her, the A12 lay quiet; never much traffic at this time of night... not that traffic was ever a problem up here. The most she was likely to encounter was a wizard heading for Lowestoft.

Past the solitary wind turbine; always good to give them a wide berth. The air turbulence could easily throw a broomstick off course.

Then the sharp left turn at Wrentham crossroads. The signpost pointing to Covehithe was small and not easily visible even on a clear night. Did these planners ever think of making them visible from above?

But she knew the route well. It was past a few straggling cottages and the house that used to be a pub when the village was a town and the road reached out to a community now lost to the sea.

Even as she soared over the rows of metal huts where the pigs were already sleeping, she could see the shadowy hulk of St Andrew's church. The oldest part of the church and the tower reached into the sky before her; the newer church nestled within its boundaries.

The first time they had met here, so long ago now, they had discovered it by accident as they swooped along the beach.

Swooped? She wondered if that was the right word. They were not the birds of prey that hovered on the clifftop, waiting for a careless sand martin to return to its nest.

No, they only came here for the drink.

Oh dear, flying creatures landing in the graveyard to drink? That made them sound like vampires. But no, there would be no blood on the old bones buried here in the last century.

Communal wine, that was the tipple of the night. They didn't call her Winey for nothing.

This snug little inner church, wrapped in the bony arms of its ancestor, was still used for services, although the whole structure was predicted to fall into the sea within the next thirty years.

'So, let's drink and be merry while we can...' She was smiling as she glided down into the rough grass, waving to her friends who had arrived first, then clutching the broomstick again as she remembered the old rule. Always better to land and wave, in that order.

These modern sticks were reputedly light and good for long journeys, but steering them with one hand... don't even ask.

'We're just waiting for Bugle,' Flute called out. 'He hasn't been here before, so he wanted to explore the building.'

Winey was always amused at the names they had given themselves. That had been a good night when they had found an old, deserted pub and discovered instruments left behind the bar. They had formed an impromptu band and played loudly and quite out of tune as the spirits went down.

No, not the kind of spirits that haunted and scared the unwary. She had been cajoled into taking a turn on one of the instruments but somehow Clarinet had not struck her as a long-term name.

Just after midnight, when someone had hauled her from a slumped position against the font, they had called in her ear 'Come on Winey, time to go,' and it had stuck. Winey she was from that night on.

'I'll meet you inside.' She was already pushing aside the first door, made of wire to keep birds out of the porch. Then the heavy wooden door creaked on its hinges, and she was in.

By the time – less than a minute later – Flute and Bugle joined her, she had already retrieved the first bottle of the red stuff from behind the heavy velvet curtain. Then Castanet joined them and the party really got going.

No-one had to be up early next morning so they indulged until a late hour, never once worrying that the bottles might be missed. After all, who was going to suspect them? They giggled as Winey put on a very formal voice and imitated a local reporting the crime. 'Oh yes, Constable, I saw them leaving. No, I didn't catch them. I couldn't reach that high.'

Then more laughter as Bugle took up the story in the same voice. 'Oh yes, Sir, there were tracks. No, not tyre tracks. More like bristles.'

The clock would have struck one if it had not fallen from the tower a century earlier. Winey had fallen asleep with her head against the hard wood of a pew.

She was dreaming and there was water lapping around her feet. Her shoes were wet, then her calves and the bottom of her cloak. She turned her shoulder away from the deluge. Where was this water coming from?

It was above her head and swirling around like a whirlpool. The noise was deafening but even above that she could hear the cracking of stone, the splintering of wooden beams, the crashing of falling masonry. She knew what it was. The ruin and the tiny church was going over the edge.

A scream escaped even as she tasted the salt water in her mouth.

'Hey, Winey. Are you ok?' Bugle and Flute and Castanet were all crouching over her.

It was dry. The stone walls still stood around her. The heavy beams still stretched above her. There was the altar and the font and the two long rows of pews.

'Ooh, sorry, I think I was dreaming.' She pulled herself up.

'I think it might be time to head home.' Flute was gathering up the empty bottles.

Winey followed them outside and they all revved up. She still felt shaken as she took off, indicating left and accelerating as quickly as she could.

'It was just a dream,' she told herself. Or was it?

The sand in her shoes and the wet cloak that drabbled around her knees made her wonder if it was more of a premonition. Would the church really be standing on this eroding cliff top for a few more years?

25 THE BEACH HUT

Gwen Bunting

Travelling overnight was easy driving for Matt. The girls were fast asleep securely tucked up on the back seat with warm blankets around them. He was pleased not to be hearing the constant, 'Are we there yet Dad?' The chorus came from the girls at almost every mile driven.

Matt was divorced from his wife, and this was his yearly holiday with the girls.

Matt and Tina had married due to a baby on the way. This was the honourable thing to do in that era. They had only been courting for 6 months when the slip-up happened; Matt was devastated. Marriage was the last thing on his mind, but he had to go through with the wedding. He felt himself very young to be tied down but, as his mother said, 'if you play with fire, you can get burnt'.

It wasn't that bad being married. Tina had kept her job until she was six months pregnant, and the pleasures of marriage had their good side. That was until another baby was on the way with barely a year between the births.

Tina resented his attentions now; she was having problems with the second pregnancy and so rebuffed Matt's demands. This brought friction between the two, hence an early separation.

He paid the maintenance weekly and had the girls stay overnight with him once a month. This restricted his social life but could have been worse if he was still married to Tina.

The small flat he rented at Southwold was expensive but, as he worked on the trawler fleet, he needed to be at the coast. The girls adored coming to see their dad as they usually spent time at the coast when the weather permitted.

Matt decided to take the girls further south to Blyth which was not so expensive and the guest houses were more plentiful. It was an old-fashioned seaside resort which Matt remembered being taken to as a child.

He found moderately priced accommodation for the two weeks in August that his boat was onshore being repaired. He had collected the girls from Norwich where they lived with their mother and her new boyfriend.

Dawn was beginning to break and the girls would soon be waking up, asking questions. The guest house he had booked was not available to new tenants till two pm so Matt had to find somewhere to while away the hours before presenting himself at the guest house.

As he drove to the beach he noticed the beach huts. They were new additions to Blyth. He parked up, and the girls woke bleary eyed asking the immortal question, 'Are we there Dad?'

Matt had spotted a café at the entrance to the beach area, and it was already open. Nice hot cup of tea and a bacon sandwich would not go amiss; the girls would be hungry too.

In the café they found a seat and eyed the menu. The girls were having poached eggs on toast and Matt his bacon buttie. There were comics for the girls to look at while Matt went outside for a smoke. On an advertising board outside the café he spied the rental of a beach hut. It was just the thing for the girls to enjoy – the beach, and somewhere to hide away should it rain. Guest houses did not encourage residents to stay in their rooms during the day, and the small lounge was full of residents anyway on wet days.

The advert for the beach hut gave a telephone number and address, which Matt noted down. He returned to the girls, saying he was just going to make a phone call. He wanted it to be a surprise.

The lady who answered the phone sounded very nice and said the chalet was free. If he would like to collect the keys and pay the fee she would be home till ten-thirty. She gave her address and directions.

On returning to the girls he told them of their new plans, and they were delighted. After Matt perused the map for directions to the address, he set off. They arrived at the road with the girls looking out for the number twenty-four.

Matt stopped and told the girls to stay in the car while he organised the paperwork and keys. Much to his surprise a voluptuous young lady answered the door, inviting him in. The rent paid for the beach hut and keys handed over, Matt was a little overawed by the female. Pulling himself together he headed off to the car and the beach hut.

The girls were delighted with the accommodation and soon set about finding buckets and spades.

Matt claimed the lounger, so he could drape his bronzed body outside for any passing female that caught his eye. Being a fisherman gave you a good tan in the summertime. He decided to change into his swimming trunks.

Closing the doors he began to undress. Suddenly, the doors flew open and the owner of the beach hut was staring at him grabbing a towel to protect his modesty. She blushed and apologised. After handing him the parking ticket for the car park near the beach, she turned and walked away sniggering.

They all enjoyed their time on the beach, especially Matt watching the talent walk by and thinking of his earlier encounter.

Arriving at the guest house at the appropriate time for new arrivals they were shown to their rooms. Matt was allocated a double as they had no single rooms available, but it was emphasised that this was a single booking, not a double.

After changing and putting their clothes away it was nearly dinner time, so they made their way towards the dining room and found their table.

As they perused the menu, the waitress approached their table. Much to Matt's astonishment it was the owner of the beach chalet!

He blushed, which was unusual for him. Managing to order their meal and concentrate on what the girls were saying, his mind kept wandering to the happenings of the afternoon.

Sarah introduced herself, asking if they had any dietary requirements and Matt's mind went into overdrive.

He managed to bumble out 'No, thanks. Nothing out of the ordinary.' To which Sarah gave a wry smile.

When dinner was over Sarah approached the table and asked if they were going into the bar as there was a film starting that she thought might engage the girls' attention.

Matt's eyes lit up. He agreed, feeling something being pushed into his hand and squeezed. Putting it into his pocket he led the girls to the lounge and bar where he indulged in a small whiskey to steady his nerves.

He was not in the habit of women approaching him. Usually it was Matt chasing the ladies.

In a quiet corner, he took the note from his pocket and read it discreetly.

'Meet me at the beach hut at nine o'clock tonight if you fancy a romantic evening. Sarah.'

Buying a bottle of wine from the bar, Matt discreetly took it to the car and hid it.

Something for later, he thought. This is going to be a great holiday.

26 SIGHT FOR SORE EYES

Val Chapman

Well, we finally made it. I never thought I would get Old Grumpy Drawers to agree to a last-minute sunshine holiday. He had been "umming" and "ahhing" for months. Always some excuse…

"Have to sort out the guttering before winter."

"The bowls club need me."

"I promised to help Ron with his car."

Anyone would think he didn't want to go on holiday with me and, to be honest, I was considering going on my own. Or even with Jenny. Although, on reflection, a holiday with my daughter wouldn't be much of a break for me.

That's the trouble with living close to grown up children: we are too convenient, always on hand for childminding duties helping out with gardening or shopping because they are "just too busy".

It's nice to be needed still, I suppose, but it really does leave me feeling exhausted and, if I am honest, a little resentful. I had no doubt she would spend the entire week complaining about the kids, her husband Craig or her job. Quite honestly, I could do without her moaning.

Which is why I was thrilled when Chuckles actually agreed to a wonderful break, and before he could say "Strawberry Daiquiri," we were soaking up the sun, listening to the waves gently breaking on the shore.

We had been on the island for two days, and to my surprise we were both having a lovely time. The hotel was very nice, right on the beach, not too busy, with gorgeous food and delicious cocktails. We hadn't ventured very far as the hotel was quite enough, but on the third day, Old Sour Puss said he fancied a walk.

I packed a few bits in my new Marks and Spencer beach bag and straight after breakfast we were off.

It really was lovely, the white promenade lined with beautiful purple bougainvillea. He even held my hand at one point.

I admit I was feeling quite giddy and young again, as it brought back memories of our first holiday together. As we took a break to sit on a bench I could tell he was thinking the same.

We shared a little kiss and carried on with our walk. In the distance we could see another beach, less populated than the one our hotel was on. The sunshine bouncing off the sea made it look like something out of a fairytale.

The heat was beginning to get to us, and my leg was playing up, so we decided to head back. Besides, it was Karaoke night, and I was determined to wow them all with my, "Fat Bottom girls."

On the way, Droopy Chops decided he would hire a car in the morning so we could explore further afield. I wasn't convinced I would be fit to explore anything after an Espresso Martini or three, but I let him have his way this time.

It was a marvellous night. I had everyone on their feet with my Karaoke favourites. and people were saying that they had never heard anything like it before!

The next day I felt surprisingly chipper and while Grumpy went to sort out the car hire I packed the bag again.

In hardly any time we had travelled almost to the other side of the island, where we stumbled on yet another beautiful beach. We decided to spend some time here, so I took the bag out of the car, picked up the towels and we made our way down through the beach grass to the pale yellow sand.

We found somewhere to sit, next to a large rock, and I decided to strip off my t-shirt and shorts, leaving just my bathing costume. The sea was too inviting so we headed towards the shore for a paddle.

As the waves gently caressed our toes, we gazed around us.

We could hear people chatting, clearly locals, and felt smug that we had found a secluded place off the beaten track, not usually frequented by tourists.

It took us a few moments to notice.

The few golden bodies that were enjoying the afternoon sun were stark naked. Had we really just hit upon a nudist beach?

Ferret Features gripped my arm.

His eyes were like saucers and, quite frankly, I wasn't surprised. There were some kids around, fair enough. There were some young people, beautiful young people, who looked like they belonged in a magazine.

And there were others, similar age to us, who were laughing and clearly loving life.

We turned and headed back towards the rock we were sitting beside, as nonchalantly as possible, our eyes fixed straight ahead.

We all but collapsed down next to the rock, trying to stifle shocked laughter. After a short while I started re-packing my bag when Mr Crabby grabbed my arm again.

Turns out he had always had a hankering to try this kind of thing.

Who knew?

After a bit of a discussion, the smooth-talking bugger somehow persuaded me that we should give it a go.

I wanted to go and think about it, but before I knew it, he had dropped his shorts and was runnin – well, walking fast – towards the water, flopping about all over the place.

Well, I wasn't having that. He wasn't the only one who could flop about. My swimming costume was discreetly discarded, my bazookas broke free from their constraints, joyous in their wild abandonment. My midriff followed suit, the rolls undulating with glee.

I confess I was nervous about revealing the next part of my anatomy. It hadn't seen the light of day for years.

I didn't move. I couldn't move. He noticed and came back for me.

Before long I found myself standing knee deep in the sea, completely nude, hand in hand with the love of my life.

He held me close and whispered to me, "We are going to need some more sun cream."

Later, at the hotel, we talked about going there again. I lay in bed wondering how I was going to lose three stone overnight, then realised that no-one knew me here. I could embrace the wonderful feeling of freedom without a care in the world.

Grumpy couldn't wait to go back and we spent most of the rest of the holiday there. It was liberating and surprisingly comfortable.

Back home, he looked for nudist beaches near us.

He has been quite a few times.

Me? In Norfolk? Not on your life!

27 SECRETS OF THE SEA

Val Fish

As I sit and watch the waves
Gently lapping against the shore
I gaze out to sea and wonder
What lies beneath?

Shipwrecks and sunken treasures?
Or mermaids, sea serpents and such?

As I sit and watch the waves
Crashing against the cliffs
I gaze out to sea and wonder
What secrets does it keep?

28 LARRY AT SEA

Laraine Newsom

Linda was furious. She had just found out that her husband Larry had purchased an inflatable diving boat. The majority of their savings were now gone.

Nevertheless, she agreed that they would go to Brighton and try out the new boat and do a bit of diving.

Before they went she insisted on getting insurance for the duration that they were away. Linda was still furious, and if he wanted to play at diving, she wanted to have security for herself. She was also a diver and so they went for a joint insurance plan at an amount of one million pounds that one of them would receive in the event of the other dying.

The cover for accidental death was for just one month. She was showing her displeasure by making him pay a large amount of money for a ridiculously short amount of time. It was her way of making a statement.

They travelled with their friends Alan and Doris who were also divers. All belonged to the same divers club. They dropped the boat off at the quay and went to the hotel to settle in before dining and drinking. The next day they were to take the boat out.

On the following day Doris decided that she would rather sunbathe on the beach. The others went out in the diving boat with Linda steering. Larry was surprised that she had gone out so far.

Alan was feeling a bit sick, so decided not to do the dive. Larry still wanted to go diving in the sea; he hoped to bring back some fish. With wet suit on, fins, mask and air bottle attached he sank into the depths.

Larry always felt comfortable in the sea, he loved diving to investigate sunken ships or just to catch fish. He had been to many different countries to indulge in such pastimes.

Linda turned to Alan and said, "Come on, let's go back to the beach for a little while and sit with Doris".

They knew Larry would stay under water as long as he could, so felt they had plenty of time. In fact, Linda was still not in the best of moods and would not care if he never resurfaced.

Once on shore they settled down and stretched out making the most of the sun.

When they went back to where they thought was the spot from which Larry had dived, they were unable to find the marker buoy.

The problem was that the tide was going one way with the wind blowing in a different direction. It's the tide that takes the diver and not the wind, but they made the mistake of following the wind, having forgotten about the tide going in the opposite direction. They eventually gave up and returned to the coast.

When Larry finally surfaced there was no boat to be seen. He wondered if he had drifted off course. He felt concerned as the air in his tank was getting low. He was a good swimmer, but the shore looked to be miles away.

He started swimming. He was a couple of miles from shore when he got cramp in his leg and started to struggle. He was picked up by another boat just as he collapsed with pain and exhaustion.

The boat was a small fishing vessel on its way to a harbour further up the coast from Brighton. By the time they got there his condition had worsened and he was taken by ambulance to Eastbourne general hospital.

As Larry was delirious, the hospital staff were concerned and they had to sedate him.

In the meantime, Alan and Doris had to return home; Alan's parents were not coping very well with their children.

They left with car and boat, expecting to meet up with Larry and Linda in a day or two.

Another day had gone by and Linda was beginning to think that Larry must have drowned. She had reported him missing, but there was no news.

Left on her own, she was thinking, thank goodness he was insured for a million pounds. She was deciding what she would do with the money.

Yes, she decided she liked the idea. They did not have any children. Larry had wanted to see more of the world before completely settling down. They got along very well. They loved one another but were not in love with each other. She decided that with one million pounds she could live without him very well.

She would cry at the funeral and then enjoy the best things that money can bring. She had resigned herself to a life without Larry.

One week later Larry was ready to leave the hospital.

He had been diagnosed with pleurisy amongst other issues. He was given the all-clear and left the hospital.

He caught a taxi which was to drop him off at the local supermarket in Brighton so that he could pick up a bottle of champagne to celebrate his recovery. Although he remained angry that his fellow divers had been negligent in not staying put, he decided that things could have been worst and there was no point dwelling on what could have happened.

He was also in the wrong; divers should never go out alone. This was a lesson that Larry would not forget.

Linda had still not heard anything and decided to go back home and arrange a meeting with a solicitor about the insurance claim. She was humming as she left the hotel.

As she was crossing the road she locked eyes with her husband who was walking towards her. Just as reality dawned on her; a car suddenly swerved and knocked her down. Larry witnessed it all.

The cause of death was injuries from the car crash. The elderly driver had had a heart attack. Both were pronounced dead upon arrival at the hospital. Larry was in shock.

Six months later, Larry received a cheque from the insurance company for one million pounds.

Coastal Tales

29 THE MARY M BERKELY

Henry Curry

Of course, we should never have been there. Now, I began to see how things were turning… well… a little tricky for us.

"Try again!" Ruary shouted, battling the sound of the wind. I pushed the lever forward and tried some revs.

"It's still no good. The prop must be fouled." Smoke was whisked away by the whirling banshee of a gale. The late afternoon glow from the shore was fading, and we could just make out the jagged teeth of the forbidding Skean Ghurr stack.

There was no doubt now. Without engine power our boat was drifting towards the very rocks we'd been warned to avoid.

Ruary McBrae is a six-foot-four tower of a Scot, all stories and laughter. My best pal. I'd known him for many years, since we'd met in London, working at the offices of an international tyre company.

Thick as thieves we were, always up to some jape, good friends from the start. Our lives and careers parted us, but we met up when we could. I knew Ruary's wife, Bid, would be waiting for us at Brannoch harbour with her two spiky little terriers, Hamish and Melise.

Talking with Bid and Ruary was always an amazing experience, powerfully good for the soul. Bid is a biologist, a painter and jazz afficionado with a razor-sharp wit. When the two of them met, we all knew here was a partnership the like of which was not repeated often.

Ruary is a polymath, polyglot and poly a lot of other things too! He is interested in just about everything, that marvellous mix of both a natural teacher and student. I once spent an hour on the train to London with this amazing couple and ended up with my chest aching from all the laughter. I should say, when Ruary laughs he throws his head back and the noise is incredible, fit to shake the sheep from the hills.

I'd come up for a long weekend to their little cottage, and after an energetic walk and a killer of a night in the bar of the local hotel, we'd been given the chance to take a boat out from Brannoch. Ruary was writing a book about the French army in World War Two and needed a break from his research. I had some spare time from my job, so his friend Jimmy said we could borrow his lovely little yacht, the *Jeannie Deans*, a twenty-foot beauty.

"Just mind you keep clear of yon Skean Ghurr and you'll be fine," Jimmy had warned.

I've sailed a lot and Ruary is plenty familiar with boats, but we obviously didn't know the ins and outs of *Jeannie*, so Jimmy took us awhile for a wee bit of practice in the safe waters inside the harbour walls. When all was fine, we put Jimmy ashore and set off south, keeping reasonably close to the coastline. It was a crackling clear blue sky afternoon with just a slight offshore breeze. We were as happy as two boys skipping school.

After a couple of hours, we turned back north, the little boat gently rocking on the negligible swell. Over a dram or two and some oatcakes we swapped stories, as ever.

"Do you remember the open day and the traffic cones?" Ruary was already laughing as we reminisced.

"You with one on your head directing, me with one on my knee as Long John road mender!"

And so the stories flowed.

A while passed and we realised we must have gone rather too far north, missing the harbour entrance. As so often happens at sea, the sky greyed over quite quickly and the wind was whipping up a hefty swell. We thought it prudent to take the sail in, relying instead on the little inboard engine, carefully turning across the waves back towards Brannoch.

There was a shudder.

"Dammit, the engine's stalled." Ruary had been at the helm and, being the engineer, I felt a bit responsible for this problem.

"We'll have fouled a line or fishing net. No mind, easily fixed."

A positive chap always, our Ruary. But despite our efforts, laughter, and a few good oaths, the engine wouldn't run. Once restarted, and as soon as I let the clutch in, it stopped again.

Now we were drifting past Bheinn M'hain, the doleful hill guarding the steep cliffs just above those fearsome rocks. We checked our mobile phones. No signal. So I fired up the VHF radio and put out a call to the coastguard, asking for help, feeling not a little foolish. After a few minutes there was a muffled reply, so I felt reassured.

"Too deep to anchor, I'm betting." Ruary was looking a bit serious.

After twenty anxious minutes or so, I was relieved to see a light approaching in the deepening gloom.

"There's a boat, we'll be okay now." Ruary grinned, with a slap on my back fit to nearly break bones, as usual. The light came closer, and we soon made out the shape and the name of the lifeboat, the *Mary M. Berkely*. The three crew on board were shouting in Gaelic but we worked out they wanted us to take a line, which we gratefully did, thanking them. Another story to tell when we get back to a nice fire and a pint or two, I thought.

The sky darkened completely now and I could barely make out our friendly lifesavers.

Rounding the outer harbour wall we reached the entrance. There was more shouting as we gently bumped the quay, and the line was gladly thrown back by Ruary.

"What have you been up to now?" Bid was smiling on the quayside, trying to stop the dogs as they jumped and yapped in greeting.

"We'll tell you all about it over a nice supper, and we could use a drink."

I winked at Ruary, already hearing him telling the well-embellished tale, in my head.

Next morning the air was a little thick after the previous night's homecoming celebrations. Jimmy had been down to the boat and taken a coil of rope from the propeller.

"My lad Stuart could have done that for you," he said, grinning.

We smiled, Stuart being all of eight years old. Ruary waved, laughing, as we walked away.

"Let's go round to the lifeboat station and give them a proper thank you, shall we?" Thoughtful as ever, he'd been up to the local shop early and bought a large pack of beer.

The RNLI building was a beautiful old stone and brick structure, sturdy yet graceful.

"Hi there, two rather embarrassed mariners, come to thank you for helping us out yesterday." A weather-beaten face grinned back at us, eyes lighting up at the sight of the beer.

"Ach, now, I was away in town at a funeral yesterday, but I'll make sure your gift goes to the team." He ushered us into the building, mostly given over to a gleaming museum, full of badges, photos, awards and memorabilia.

"The Shannon class in the harbour is a fine ship, she is. Where was it that the lads picked you up?"

"We were just off Skean Ghurr when the *Mary M. Berkely* came to us, and very pleased to see her we were!"

I shook his hand, but his expression changed and he drew back.

"You must be mistaken."

Ruary sensed the change in atmosphere and smiled. "Well, we're most grateful."

The old boy looked thoughtful. "Come with me." He stopped, turning to look me in the eye. "The *Mary M. Berkely* you say?" I nodded, bemused. We followed him further into the building to a much bigger room that held just a large boat, its shiplap planking bearing an ugly gash down one side. He turned again and spoke quietly.

"Yesterday I was at the funeral of Ian Muir, coxswain here for some forty years. Ninety he was, a tower of a man. He was the only survivor from the 1973 disaster when our boat went out to a trawler that was in difficulties off the Skean Ghurr stack.

"Two lads were lost that day – fifty years ago. Yesterday was the anniversary. Old Ian's last words, so it was told to me, were that he'd like to be out again, out for just one more shout, helping one last ship in distress."

During this little speech we'd been working our way round to the front of the preserved vessel. Its name was beautifully picked out in gold lettering.

"The *Mary M. Berkely* took to the rocks herself and was badly damaged. But she was saved and brought back here to the museum, as a memorial to those lads."

I looked at Ruary, who was stroking his beard, deep in thought.

30 SEAL SKIN

Val Chapman

Ursula sat on the garden bench gazing out to sea. She found herself increasingly drawn to this spot. Her mother had been so proud of the garden. She remembered her mother spending hours out here, digging and planting till well after dusk.

The last thing she had put into the garden was the bench.

Made from bits of driftwood collected from the beach and built by her parents, it was her mother's pride and joy. When the weather was kind, the two of them would sit here, Ursula listening intently to the seafaring tales her mother loved to tell, or reading a book about life in the sea.

When her brother Alex arrived, he would be wrapped tightly in a soft, knitted shawl and he too would join them on the bench.

Ursula sighed.

She missed her mum so much.

Alex was old enough now to go out on the boats with Dad, but he and his friend Robbie were talking about running a cycle hire business for the tourists. They spent most of their time planning trails around

Orkney, Hoy, and a few of the other neighbouring islands.

Ursula was still trying to find out where she fitted in.

When she left school she started work in the Harbour Restaurant. She hadn't been there long before she realised it wasn't right for her. Luckily, she managed to land a job with The Highland Park distillery and felt much more settled.

Now though, Ursula had found somewhere else which suited her more.

The Neolithic Village of Skara Brae was just a short drive away from home.

Known to pre-date the Egyptian Pyramids, it was becoming more and more popular with tourists and last year they had over 100,000 visitors. Ursula was part of the team tasked with the upkeep of the visitor centre.

It wasn't a difficult job by any means, and sometimes a few of the archaeologists would take her on site, knowing how interested she was in the islands' history.

There were a surprising number of visitors to Orkney these days with May and September being the busiest. It was probably because they were the drier months, but people would always show up to spot the seals, whales, porpoises and otters.

Ursula wasn't in the least surprised. It didn't matter how often she caught a glimpse of an orca or a seal, it still sent a thrill through her. She was becoming as obsessed by the sea as her mother was.

Was?

For all she knew, her mother was still out there somewhere, completely oblivious to the fate and lives of her children.

Ursula had spent years regretting telling her mother about the sealskin she found in the loft of Tam's boat shed.

It was, she now knew, the catalyst her mother had been searching for.

She had been told tales – of course she had. Places like this were full of weird and wonderful folklore stories.

One of her favourites had been the stories about the Selkies, or Selkie-wives. Seals that would come to shore, take off their seal skins and become human women. They would marry and have children, who would invariably have webbed fingers, toes, or both.

There would remain in them a longing to return to the sea, and the man they married would hide their skin to keep them with him.

Whenever the Selkie was ready to return, all she needed to do was put her sealskin back on.

If she could find it.

Such tales fascinated Ursula, so when she had gone with her father to the boatyard and discovered an old wooden chest, her curiosity was piqued.

She could hardly wait to tell her mother, thinking it could be the skin from a selkie-wife.

If she had thought for one moment it belonged to her own mother, she might have kept quiet.

Ursula could not be sure how long it was after the discovery that her mother disappeared, but it seemed only a matter of days.

Her father and Alex, while shocked, seemed to accept the situation relatively quickly, Ursula was devastated for the longest time.

She had been just seven years old. She needed her mum.

She grew up, becoming increasingly distant from her father and brother. Several opportunities to leave Orkney came her way in recent years, but how could she?

What if her mother returned?

So, she continued to sit on the garden bench, gazing out to sea, watching the seals.

Glancing down at her webbed toes, she lifted her head again, looked out and wondered.

31 THE LAST LAUGH

Hilary Woodjets

'Bobby?'

I sighed.

'Bobby? Bobby, is that you? Effin 'ell, time ain't bin too good to yer, 'as it, gal?'

'Hello, Josie. How nice to see you.'

People were turning to look at us; the quiet, mousey woman with her long hair hiding her face who had been silently reading her book a few moments ago, and the blowsy caricature who sat beside her, face reddened from her coughing fit.

Josie had always been a good-looking woman, well suited to the life of a professional escort. When she wanted to, she was every bit as capable of sounding like the member of the aristocracy she pretended to be, instead of the scavenging working class pickpocket she actually was.

We met in a bar one night after she had finished 'work', got talking and discovered a common interest. We both quite liked relieving the rich of their possessions and redistributing them to the poor.

That is, to ourselves.

For a number of years, our modus operandi didn't change. Josie would enter any hotel that looked as though it had a rich clientele, cosy up to the concierge, and tell them she was 'available to entertain the gentlemen guests'.

Some nights, she would get lucky and just get taken to dinner as arm candy, go back to a man's room, have a chat, and slip a little something into his nightcap. When he was asleep before the action he hoped would start, she would strip him of his watch and his wallet, and even his wedding ring and gold cufflinks.

Other times, she was prepared to go the whole distance, which is where I would come in.

It was difficult with the odd mark who was teetotal. We couldn't slip anything into his coffee because the taste would tell, and on one occasion we were nearly rumbled. But then I arrived as 'housekeeping' with fresh towels, and while she was trying to placate the man and tell him nothing was untoward, I excused myself and put the towels in the en suite, save for the flannel I kept in a pocket along with cable ties.

Once the man had succumbed to the mesmerising charms on top of him, swinging in his face while she pushed his wrists up to the bedstead, I loomed into his view, snapped a cable tie around his wrist and the bed head, and stuffed the flannel in his mouth before he finished drawing breath to shout.

Meanwhile, she put the other cable tie on his other wrist. Then we took the curtain tiebacks from their holders to bind his wrists and feet more securely, removing the cable ties so that when he was discovered next day and the real housekeeping staff got over their shock and their giggles, nothing would seem odd other than he had been a bit of a naughty boy.

It was a common enough occurrence for it to remain a secret that, while he was helplessly watching, we had relieved him of much of his worldly wealth – that which he carried with him, anyway.

He was hardly going to tell anyone, was he?

Josie knew a couple of fences, who were capable of getting stuff out on the market, or even out of the country if need be and, for a while, this practice did very well for us. We split the profits.

Then we took it up a notch. Hotel concierges can be both your best friends and your worst enemies; it depends on your point of view.

Honest ones are a pain, because they will call the police while you are still selling your pitch to them. Dishonest ones are also a pain; they want a piece of the action, otherwise they will also call the police.

The end result is pretty much the same: blues and twos, ' 'Ello, 'ello, 'ello; wot 'ave we got 'ere, then?' Swiftly followed by 'You're nicked!' And a nice, comfy ride to the cells.

If we were lucky – and depending on our acting skills and sob story of the night – we might get let off with a smacked wrist by a station sergeant on the graveyard shift who was too freakin' knackered, too busy or too lazy to deal with the paperwork involved. Or a combination of all three.

If we weren't, it was a night in the cells, court in the morning and then either probation or a short sentence. We were too clever by half to get more than one or two of those, mind you.

So, we had the idea of leaving the concierges out of the loop and loitering in the lobbies and hallways to watch the housekeeping staff at work. We'd choose the ones who didn't look happy in their work, watch them to see why they weren't happy – usually because they were being bullied by the head housekeeper – and see if they wanted to make a bit of money on the side by giving us information.

In case you don't know, chambermaids are often foreigners sending money back home out of their meagre (often less than) minimum wage, and they have no more than twenty minutes to clean each room. Once they have proved they can do that, their time gets cut to fifteen minutes, and they get allotted another couple of rooms on top. So be nice to them when you next stay in a hotel and give them a good tip other than 'get another job' when you leave. Otherwise....

Her name was Sofia. She was a lovely girl but often looked as though she had been crying. I asked her whether she liked working at the Grand, and she burst into tears and a flood of Spanish.

I speak a little Spanish, enough to get by, so I found out that the housekeeper was a devil in human form, who wasn't fit to work with anyone. Then I'd asked her about the guests on her floor. Were they nice to her? Were they staying long? Did they have a closet full of nice clothes for going to the opera, the theatre, or a high-class restaurant? Did they have automobile keys with a fob that said RR, Bugatti, or Aston Martin, rather than Rover, Bentley or (so help us) Mini? Not that I have anything against the latter, they are, of course, good automobiles, but not the status symbol your average tax-dodger likes to flaunt.

By the time we had chatted and I had surreptitiously helped her carry out her tasks, I would find out when she was off-duty, give her some 'sympathy money' to have a good time with her boyfriend on her day off, and then Josie and I would strike.

It wouldn't do to get our informant into trouble if she were suspected of doing anything. Nor, in fact, if she suspected *us* of nefarious practice in asking seemingly innocuous questions dropped into conversation.

Add Rosita (The Palace Hotel), Juanita (The Corona), and Giovanna (The Golden Plaza) to the mix, and we were kept meaningfully employed most days by blending in with the normal staff routines, 'borrowing' uniforms from laundry dump baskets and carefully avoiding the areas we knew we might be spotted.

The one thing we couldn't get hold of were the keys. Nowadays, hotels don't need to issue them because of electronic locks, but back in the day when we were operating you needed a good, solid key.

Once in the room which the guests (but not their belongings) had vacated, it was a simple enough matter to go through the place methodically, and to crack the in-room safe.

You know you can set your own combination on them, right? Well, think of the number of times they have to be reset so that the next guest can put their own combination into use. Thousands of times. Once your clever thief masters that art, well, you might as well leave the things open with a note on the door saying, 'come and get it'.

So we did – go and get it, I mean. Several (hundreds of) times. And always the haul was worth the effort. From jewellery, passports, wedding rings (from men who needed to pretend they 'weren't married any longer') to small antique pieces. Even a Fabergé egg on one occasion, which was too distinctive to take. Boxed diamond engagement rings we left behind, for the most part. The poor schmucks who were going to surprise their ladies with a proposal didn't need the heartache of loss, and the lucky recipient, if she didn't turn out to be all that lucky, could sell it for compensation when he went off with another woman.

Who says thieves don't have hearts? Some of us do.

Anyhoo, greed set into Josie's wretched black heart. One night we were leaving our most recent place of work, where we had come away with an astounding haul, and she turned to me and, quite without warning, shoved me into the road.

It was just my luck that the last bus of the night was trundling along at the time, and I fell against its side, getting my face lacerated, my arm broken, and a couple of ribs cracked.

She grabbed the bag with everything in it and screamed, 'See ya, sucker!' as she ran off down the road, laughing.

I was too stunned and in too much pain to move. The bus driver got off the bus, ashen-faced, and told someone to ring for the police and an ambulance.

I don't remember much after that, except that when I came round after the anesthetic they must have given me as pain relief while they examined me at the hospital, I was shackled to the bed in cuffs and told I had confessed to being 'a very naughty girl.' Apparently I had some evidence on me to corroborate that.

Long story short, I did the crime and paid the time: ten years for the accumulated offences I had committed.

I had no idea where Josie went. I later gathered she'd gone abroad for a while.

I did, however, manage to sue the bus company for the poor upkeep of their bus. That handed me a fair bit because I needed reconstructive surgery, and the police never found where I hid some of the money from our exploits, so not all of it was confiscated. Enough remained to buy me some seclusion in a clifftop residence overlooking the sea. I'm not going to give you the location, because I live a quiet life, people have stopped staring at my scarred face and I don't need sightseers.

Hence my reserved reaction and inward horror when Josie strolled into our local pub. We made nice for a while, and she had several more drinks, rendering her almost incapable. I asked her where she was staying, and she mentioned a hotel not too far from where I lived.

So, about one-thirty in the morning, we took a leisurely stroll along the cliff top walk. By this time, she was slurring her speech quite badly.

'Bobby… Bobby… I jush wanna lie down.'

I kept on walking with my arm around her, holding her up. 'Not far now, Josie.'

'Bobby… pleeease, lemme lie down. I feel… eeurgh… I think I'm gunna be shick.'

So I let her down gently. 'Oh… thash nice o' you. I like you, Bobby. Even though you're an American.'

I kept quiet for a moment. 'Josie, you do know my name is not Bobby, don't you?'

'Yer….whassamatter, yatellin' me yadoan' like it?'

'I guess I got used to it, but I never knew why you started calling me that. If my name was Roberta, I could understand it. But my name is Rachel Millicent Jones-Whitely. And you know that.'

'Ooooh, get you…. Yer was jush little Milly Jones when I knew ya.' She giggled and burped. The foul stench of her breath was staggering. 'Sorry… So, you remember when we started -.ooh I don't feel sho good – knocking off the Grand? And we didn't have any keysh?'

She groaned and rolled over a bit. 'Yer'darst me for a coupla – oh, God, I feel awful – bobby-pins… out of my hair so you could… pick the locks. I didden know what bobby-pins were until you took the hair-grips out of my hair. It jush… shtuck, I s'pose.' She closed her eyes. 'We made a good team… didden we, Bobby?'

I looked around. There was no-one walking on the cliff to help. I bent down towards her.

'My name was never Bobby. I never liked being called Bobby. I am Rachel Millicent Jones-Whitely, and Mr Whitely, who can see past my scars and doesn't know about my past, is waiting for me at home. So I'll say good night to you, and hope you rest in peace.'

With that, I gave her drunkenly stupefied form a gentle shove over the edge of the clifftop. I watched her body bounce off the rocks with a sickening crunch and come to a stop on the rocks below, battered and bleeding. Her eyes stared up at me, unseeing in death.

'See ya, sucker.'

And I went home, laughing.

As she had done when she pushed me that night so long ago.

32 A SERIAL KILLER ON CROMER PIER

Henry Curry

A serial killer on Cromer Pier
Was believed to be causing some strife
Using cudgel and gun, explosives and snakes,
Poisoned ale and a curvy cheese knife.

The serial killer on Cromer Pier
Had mastered the art of disguise.
He could merge into backgrounds, resemble a fish,
A book or some doubtful meat pies.

That serial killer on Cromer Pier
Was given to parallel parking.
He jumped from his car, throttled old Freddie Starr,
Three nuns and a salesman from Barking.

As the serial killer on Cromer Pier
Used his cunning to get a lot nearer
For Health and for Safety the management said
"We'll make the front rows ten pounds dearer."

This serial killer on Cromer Pier
Had despatched almost all of the cast
Of the pantomime, first came the cat and the dame,
The conductor and orchestra last.

Coastal Tales

No serial killer on Cromer Pier
Had ever amassed such a killing.
So the local police were amazed and in awe
And had given this blackguard top billing.

But the serial killer on Cromer Pier
Must slip; they were sure his addiction
To murder may lead to the subtlest clue
Which could lead to arrest and conviction.

"Stop the Serial Killer on Cromer Pier!"
Screamed the headlines; the public were fearful
That he would pop up as they scoffed their ice creams
With a ripple they all became tearful.

Then the serial killer on Cromer Pier
Made an error, his copybook blotted
Seen by a bold usher, seat 17A
Was where this dark villain had squatted.

"They've caught the killer on Cromer Pier!"
Shouted onlookers, "He looks downhearted."
He squirmed and he wriggled against the strong hands
Seems his fight to survive had departed.

Now the serial killer on Cromer Pier
Took a regular diet, most wonderful:
Chillies, garlic and prunes, baked beans and macaroons.
His intestinal tract was quite thunderful.

Coastal Tales

Was the serial killer on Cromer Pier
At last to be brought to trial?
No, he'd gone – and was never to be seen again.
All he left was an odour most vile.

33 JURRASSIC COAST

Stephen Oliver

The cliff was more majestic than I expected and took me back in time.

Literally.

That's the problem with Chronos Syndrome; you're unstable in the temporal dimension. Worse, there's little you can do about when you'll end up unless you're an Alpha, or a Primary like me, where you have total control of your talent, including when you go and when you travel to.

Even so, the timefold sometimes catches you unawares, and you're swept off into the timestream, out of control.

That's what happened.

My parents were holidaying on the Jurassic Coast in southern England. I dropped in to visit over the weekend after a week's training in my new abilities with my Great-Grandfather.

I hadn't had them a month before, but with a bit of judicious temporal tinkering, we'd managed to give ourselves these abilities. The thing is, we had evidence that we'd both been born Primaries, and someone had manipulated the past to stop us by removing them.

So, we manipulated it back again!

Coastal Tales

And our enemies hadn't realised we'd done it, either.

As I came out of the timefold, I looked around.

Fortunately, with my newly acquired abilities, I no longer feel disorientated and dizzy during transitions, or for a short while after arrival. Timedrop sickness, we call it.

I'd been walking along the beach on a lovely sunny day, but now, it was cold and gusty. In the distance out to sea, I could see a thunderstorm receding, the clouds still flickering occasionally with sheet lightning. The cliffs to my right were somewhat closer than before, letting me know I'd travelled a couple of centuries into the past, during which they'd been weathered.

I pulled my smart phone out. The Temporal Shifter's Organisation had provided it, and it is much more than just the usual type you can buy in any shop.

There's a series of geosynchronous satellites circling the planet in Clarke orbits. Three Alphas went up in the space shuttle and jumped back to place them there 100,000 years ago, at the utmost limit of their abilities. They're there to help temporal shifters orientate themselves as quickly as possible through the SatLink in the phones.

It told me I had arrived late in 1811, the year before Napoleon's famous defeat.

I gazed around, wondering what I was supposed to do here.

You see, I've discovered that there's no coincidence about when you end up when it's a random journey. There's always a reason, no matter how strange that might seem. It's as if someone is moving us around through time, playing a game of 5D chess.

"Good day, kind sir," said a young girl's voice behind me. "I did not see you before, for my gaze was solely on these fascinating bones."

I turned around to discover a young girl, possibly pre-teen, with long dark hair blowing back from her face in the stiff breeze.

"Bones, young lady?" I asked. "Surely you mean 'stones'?"

"No, Sir. 'Bones.'"

She held out three small greyish items in her palm.

"Touch them," she encouraged me. "Feel them. See how they have a different texture from all the stones here."

I reached out and touched them.

A shock ran up my arm into my head.

Actually, it was a double shock.

I felt the age of the items in a way I'd never felt before. Somehow, I was aware of the extreme number of years since they had been part of a living being, like a vast weight pressing down on my soul.

Then, I felt a terrible drag to go back along their timeline to the time they were still alive.

Fortunately, I was able to resist the second shock because that temporal span was way beyond my abilities.

"Are you well, sir?" the girl asked. "You became quite white."

I shook off the shocks.

"I'm fine, young lady. What is your name?"

"My name is Mary Anning. I live nearby."

I told her my name as we walked parallel to the cliffs.

"What do you think they are bones of?" I asked her.

"I know not, sir, for I am not widely read. But I believe they are called 'fossils' and come from creatures from long before the Great Flood."

"Is that so?" I asked. "Why do you believe so?"

"Why, they are hard as stone but still resemble bones. It must take ages upon ages to harden bone this way."

"I grant you must be right."

Her eyes were on the stones and rocks we passed over, darting hither and yon as she sought more fossils.

We walked for over five minutes before I felt that strange double shock again: immense age and a drag toward something. Only this time, it wasn't along a timeline, but instead to my right.

"What on earth?" I muttered to myself.

"What is it, sir?" Mary asked.

"Something in the cliff caught my eye for a moment. I have no idea what it is."

"Shall we search for it?"

"Of course."

I set up, letting myself follow the unknown force dragging me forward.

Soon, we stood before the cliff.

From the fresh rocks scattered at our feet, it was evident that there had been a rockfall during the stormy night. Something large and white stuck out of the cliff, definitely the remains of a once-living thing.

"I believe this is the head of a... krakodile," Mary said with some hesitation.

"I think the word you're looking for is 'crocodile'," I said.

She glanced up at me.

"You may be right, sir. As I said, I am not well read."

"But you are an intelligent and observant young lady."

She blushed.

I stared at the fossil. It resembled no crocodile or alligator I had ever seen before. It appeared more fish-like due to its flattened sides.

She touched it for a moment before turning back the way we had come. Putting her hands to her mouth, she shouted at the top of her lungs.

"Joseph. Joseph. Come and see what we've found!"

A young man, a couple of years older than her, ran around the headland.

"What is it, Mary?" he cried as he approached us, throwing me a suspicious glance.

"Look," she said, pointing at our find. "A big fossil."

He threw me another glance, this time a relieved one, before staring down at the fossil.

"Oh," he said. "Is that a krakodile?"

"This gentleman says it is pronounced 'crocodile', Joseph."

"I think it might be a fish," Joseph said.

Mary peered more closely.

"I believe you may be right."

She looked up at her brother, her eyes bright.

"I believe we have an ancient fish."

"Yes, you are right," Joseph replied.

They grinned at one another.

"Come," Joseph shouted. "We must tell Mother and Father." With that, he began to run back the way he had come.

"Thank you, kind sir," Mary said and squeezed my hand for a moment before taking off after her brother.

As they ran off, I decided that now was an appropriate point to timefold back to my present.

When I returned to my parents' house, I spent some time researching Mary Anning online.

It appeared that she and her brother discovered a complete ichthyosaur skeleton when she was but twelve years old. They went on to find a complete plesiosaur skeleton a decade later, as well as the first partial pterosaur remains in England.

I sat back and considered this.

Had I helped her make the discovery by changing the past? Or had I confirmed the past, ensuring the beginning of palaeontology?

And what about the feeling I'd recently had, that someone or some group were manipulating me and others toward some particular end?

In the end, I decided to wait and see. However, I felt compelled to glance up into the air and speak to no one.

"I don't know what your plans are, but as long as they are for the good of all humanity, I'll let you continue to use me and my abilities. Okay?"

Of course, there was no reply, but I hadn't expected one.

34. THE VAN

Our much-loved member, Jan Cunningham, died in 2024. Not only was she the guiding force behind the formation of the Whittlesey u3a, she was an early member of the creative writing group, which became Whittlesey Wordsmiths.

Those of us who knew Jan, loved her, and she is sadly missed. As this book is dedicated to her memory, it seems appropriate to include one of her short stories, not on a coastal theme but one that embodies her spirit.

34 THE VAN
Jan Cunningham

The transit turned onto the trunk road, heading away from the housing estate.

Well, where are we going now? Off to his mates, I'll bet. He does my head in. Accelerator, brake, accelerator, brake, what a way to drive. He has no consideration for my suspension or tyres. Why he's in such a hurry to get to heaven is beyond my comprehension.

Still, anything's better than being stuck in his driveway, staring at the garage door all night. When his dad's at home there isn't room for two on the driveway so he leaves me in the residents' car park, next to a snazzy little red number. She's a cutie.

My driver is a plumber: young, flash, and thinks he's god's gift. The way he treats me is nigh-on criminal: hardly puts any petrol in – tight git. I'm gasping my last when he finally takes me to a petrol station.

And – talkabout speed – he thinks he's Lewis Hamilton. He forgets I'm getting on a bit and it fair takes the fumes out of my exhaust.

It was all right at first; he just used me for work. Loaded up his gear and off we went to various jobs and, I have to give it to him, he's a hard worker.

Then he started racing. He and his mates would go up on the waste ground next to the old quarry; take turns racing their vans against each other and bet on the results. Well, that wasn't in my contract. I ask you, at my age. Some nights, by the time they're finished I wish I'd gone to the scrapyard.

Now, here's the thing: I overheard them talking the other night, but I couldn't quite make out what it was about. I heard the word Derby, but that didn't mean anything to me... then.

The next thing I knows he's got a new van and I'm being shuffled off to his mates' workshop. I'm scared now as I don't trust those three idiots and they keep referring to a paper that appears to be instructions.

For what, I'd like to know?

Well, I didn't have to wait long. Next evening after work, they started ripping out all my interior, then removing headlights, tail-lights, all the plastic, trim and lastly the glass.

What's going on?

I was naked as a new model on the assembly line. If I could have crossed my wheels, I would have. I was so embarrassed, but they didn't give a hoot – just kept reading out instructions and laughing.

Next, they cut out my front and rear fenders – apparently to stop my tyres from getting cut. (Who's going to cut me?)

They cut a hole in my bonnet to allow easy access for putting out fires. (Who's going to set fire to me?) Then to crown it all they took off the driver's door, filled it with cement and put it back. This is to protect the driver from hits. (Who's going to hit him?)

They think it's such a hoot, threatening to come back the night after to finish me off.

If he'd put any petrol in me, I would have done a runner I can tell you, but as he hadn't….

The three of them returned next evening, armed with paint, brushes, and cans of spray-paint.

Now what are they up to?

They painted my driver's door black with a large number three in white. This was apparently to identify the driver. Then an argument started as to what I would be called, and which colours would be used. My choice would have been "Nutters", but they ignored me and settled on "Three Musketeers" with green and yellow for colours.

After they finished making me look a right prat, they sauntered off down to their local nearby for what they called "a well-earned bevvy", leaving me to ponder on what was coming next.

And I wasn't looking forward to it whatever it was.

On Sunday morning, I'm driven onto a low-loader. What the hell is going to happen to me?

I haven't a clue as we bowl along the country roads, sun shining, blue sky and the smell of fresh-mown grass. Normally I would have enjoyed a run in the country but not today.

I'm scared.

Eventually we turn off onto a wide track and pull up next to a field. There are concrete blocks laid in a circle, making a wide ring with cars revving and roaring around the middle of this muddy patch. I watch the goings-on in horror.

They were skidding around, bashing and crashing into each other, engines smoking, car bumpers flying and even wheels coming off. The large crowd watching egged the drivers on, shouting encouragement and whooping with delight at the antics in the arena. The noise was deafening, and I could smell fumes from the vehicles mixed in with all the other smells: BBQ, hot dogs, beefburgers... nauseating.

Was this to be my end? After years of loyal service, am I to be bashed, crashed, skidded into, and torn apart just for the fun of it?

If I'd had any screen wash left, I would have cried.

As the day wore on I began to hope, but then came the announcement I had been dreading.

"Now folks, the last event of the Demolition Derby is for vans. So would all the competitors line up in the ring."

So this was it. My end.

My driver put on his brand-new, fancy crash helmet and gloves, got in the cab, and off we went. We lined up in the ring with bonnets facing the crowd and rear ends to the middle.

"Ready? Five, Four, Three, Two, One. Crash and Bash!"

Every one drove backwards into the middle and rammed each other. Ouch! Oye! Mind out! But my cries were to no avail.

OK, if this is my finale let's make it a goodun.

We pushed, shoved, rammed... sideways on, rear to rear, bonnet to bonnet. It seemed that the only rule was do-not-hit-the-driver's-side-full-on-deliberately – otherwise, go for it.

And we did. My driver was pumped-up: yelling and whooping, spinning me round, hurtling backwards and forwards. One van's engine caught fire, so we had to stop for a few minutes while it was dealt with. One down, five to go.

Then two vans clashed head on so badly they couldn't separate so that was them done for.

Three down, three to go.

By now, the noise from the crowd was deafening, smoke pouring out from the engines, dust swirling in clouds and enveloping the ring, making it difficult to see clearly.

My cocky young driver was having a ball. He drove me hard and fast, and although I was dented, battered, and nearly buggered, we still managed to skid, turn on a sixpence and get some decent rams in. But no-one left was going to roll over easily.

The battle was fierce.

Then the number 101 van, with Suky written on the side, shunted the other van so hard it finished up straddling the concrete barrier, rocking backwards and forwards, wheels spinning frantically but unable to get back on the track.

Four down. Just the two of us left.

I just wanted the whole miserable charade to end.

Death by a thousand dents. My bodywork was crushed, wheels dented and wobbly, back and front bumpers hanging off, and bonnet knocked up.

I'd had enough. I was knackered.

Then Suky seemed to come out of nowhere and shunted me so hard I went into a wild spin.

But my driver wasn't taking that. He reversed quickly and hit Suki hard on the passenger side. The van went up and teetered, nearly going over, but just managing to right itself in time for our next belt.

This time we pushed Suki right tight to the concrete slabs. I was hoping that was it… but no. Suki managed to skitter away and drove to the far end of the arena.

My driver turned me to face the van. With both engines revving hard we set off.

If I'd had any eyes to close, they would have been shut tight as we hurtled towards each other. There was an almighty bang as we clashed bonnet to bonnet and both front ends went up into the air. For a split second, we must have looked like two boxing kangaroos: fronts in the air at a forty-five degree angle, wheels spinning and engines screamimg.

Then it was over. Suki went over backwards but we came down onto our front wheels.

We had won.

My driver was up on what was left of my bonnet; jumping up and down, fist punching the air. The crowd were clapping and cheering as he was crowned the winner and given a bottle of some cheap fizz to squirt over all and sundry.

Well, bully for us.

Thank God it's over. Right now, the scrap yard looks rather inviting. I mean, I've had a long career, not done too badly with drivers, and we've all got to go sometime – right?

Then I overheard my driver and his mates talking. It seems they are thinking of patching me up and doing it all again!

Noooooooooooooooooooooooooo....

The End

Coastal Tales

ABOUT THE AUTHORS
The Whittlesey Wordsmiths

We are a u3a (university of the 3rd age) creative writing group who meet monthly to share ideas and support each other. You can find your local UK u3a branch at https://www.u3a.org.uk/

Follow our blog at https://whittleseywordsmiths.com or email us at whittleseywordsmiths@gmail.com

Wendy Fletcher

Wendy was the original group leader of the Whittlesey Wordsmiths. After seven years, she handed over to our new leader, Henry Curry, earlier this year. She continues to be a group member and contributes to our homeworks and anthologies.

Her first book, The Railway Carriage Child (available from Amazon) is a memoir of her childhood in the Cambridgeshire Fens, growing up in two Great Eastern Railway carriages.

Wendy now gives talks across East Anglia about this experience and displays a collection of artefacts at local events. She has also had poetry published in *The Poet* magazine and short stories published on Marsha Ingrao's, *Always Write* blog. You can read more of Wendy's poems and stories in anthologies from the Whittlesey Wordsmiths

Coastal Tales

Valerie Fish

Born and bred in London, Valerie now lives in the Fens with her husband of forty-five years. She has been writing on and off for most of her adult life. Now retired, she has more time to devote to her passion, with renewed enthusiasm since joining her local u3a creative writing group. She calls herself a 'Three in the morning writer', as it's often when tossing and turning in the early hours that inspiration comes, and stories develop.

As well as limericks, she enjoys writing flash fiction, particularly fifty- or one hundred-worders, regularly contributing to online challenges and having snippets published in the *Daily Mail*. Her book, A Sexagenarian From Smithy Fen, and Other Limericks, is now available from Amazon. Find Valerie's blog online at: https://sexegenarianscribbler.wordpress.com/

Val Chapman

Having won a national essay competition at junior school in the North-East, Val decided to quit while she was ahead.

Life then got in the way and, with no prior experience, she thought she would pop along to her local u3a writing group on a whim and loved it.

It has taken her sixty years to start this writing lark. It might take her another sixty to get the hang of it.

Aside from this new-found hobby, Val loves animals, cake, and her family. Sometimes in that order.

Coastal Tales

Stephen Oliver

Stephen was utterly sane until he was born to totally normal parents. Having been precipitated into this insane world without his permission, he decided that the only logical response was to become crazy.

He hid the craziness successfully while at school. However, when he started working, he came to believe he could speak to machines. The only possible solution was to train to be a software developer.

After more than three decades of this, he completely lost his mind and decided to become a writer. Over one and a quarter million words later, he's seen the publication of fifteen short stories, a dark urban fantasy anthology (*Paranormal City*), and a space opera novel (Shuttlers) in a single year. He's now madly working on another twenty-one books, some ready for publication, the rest still being written.

He says he'll only stop writing when they peel his cold, dead fingers off the keyboard. "Mind you," he quips, "knowing the kinds of stories I write, it'll be one of my own creations that does me in!"

His present philosophy is, "Only those crazy enough to believe they'll succeed, will!"

You can follow his lunatic rantings at www.stephenoliver-author.com and on Twitter @authorstepheno

Philip Cumberland

Philip is possibly the oldest paperboy in Whittlesey and the Fens. In many ways that sums him up: he hasn't moved on much in many ways since his teens.

Born in 1951 in Paxton, he grew up in Huntingdon, spending his working life involved in the motor trade and engineering, the last thirty years of his working life running a small business.

For years, Philip has been fascinated with improving his art of writing but like many people didn't pursue his dream until later in life. A vivid imagination and the ability to inject humour into his writing are indicative of his youthful mind. He has been published in *Best of British* magazine, penned a variety of short stories, some of which are featured in this book, and published his debut novel, *Killing Time in Cambridge*, available from Amazon.

When he puts his pen down, Philip enjoys the Fens, music, reading, walking, cycling and being a general nuisance, according to his wife. Find Phil online at https://fenlandphil.com/tag/fenland/

Laraine Newson

Many years ago, Laraine loved writing stories in her English lessons at school. Then life got in the way, during which she got a honours degree. After that she found it hard to get back to 'normal' reading books. Eventually, she got back her love of reading but the icing on the cake for her was joining the Whittlesey Wordsmiths creative writing group and seeing her own little stories in this our very own book.

Jane Pobgee

Jane inherited her love of reading and storytelling from her mother, who would keep her daughters entertained for hours. Jane, in turn, made up stories for her own sons and later her granddaughters. A talk by the

Coastal Tales

Whittlesey Wordsmiths at the library encouraged her to go along to a meeting and have a go.

In the intervening years, she has added drawing to her achievements, illustrating a number of the Wordsmiths' books.

Whilst they say everyone has a book in them, she feels she has a large collection of short stories. As her characters lead her stories wherever they want to go, she is looking forward to reading them.

Hilary Woodjetts

Hilary has had fourteen jobs in her working life, ranging from social work, guide at a Victorian working museum (where she learned to make plaster casts, dip candles, and black-lead cast iron fires), guide at a water and sewage treatment works (where she learned that some people really do want their false teeth back after they've been dropped down the loo), newsagent, bus driver, and – after a few other things as well – finally ended up as a University Chapel Verger.

Not having had a career as such, Hilary says she has never been rich, but never been bored, either. She enjoys music (and was a pianist and church organist before her eyesight went wonky), reading, writing, but not 'rithmetic; travel, camping, and spending time with her long-suffering husband and their cat, who hitched a lift from France in the engine bay of their motor home in 2008. (The cat, that is. Not the husband.)

Henry Curry

Henry retired in 2015 from a long career in telecoms with BT and Nokia. Born into a large family in Tottenham, North London, he has lived in Whittlesey since 1988 with his talented wife. In 1984, he gained a degree in science and technology from the Open University and followed this up with an uncompleted MSc in entomology. (He swears he will resume this, one day.)

In the mid-1990s, he and his wife were in a team of volunteers that set up and ran the National Dragonfly Museum at Ashton Mill in Northamptonshire and, five years later, the Dragonfly Project at Wicken Fen in Cambridgeshire. He became secretary of the British Dragonfly Society in 2006 and served on their Board of Trustees for thirteen years.

Among his interests, Henry loves writing, classical music, computing, aeroplanes, buses, railways, photography, science, a bit of drawing, and natural history. For the last forty years or so, he has been madly passionate about insects, and dragonflies in particular.

Henry spends time studying, travelling, walking, trying to play golf, and writing. He began writing classes at City College in Peterborough in 2016 under the excellent tutorship of Tim Wilson and has been writing ever since. Since 2016, he has been on the committee of NAWG (the National Association of Writing Groups).

When not writing, Henry spends far too much time just staring at the wonders in his garden pond.

Gwen Bunting

As a schoolgirl, Gwen always liked writing compositions, whatever they are called these days. Later in life, joining a Writing Group and being encouraged by the leader but not by some members of the group, she plodded on.

Coastal Tales

Whittlesey Wordsmiths is Gwen's 4th writing group she has joined and enjoys most of the topics set. Gwen has had a varied life, travelling to various places in the world during the years her husband served in the RAF. Now retired, Gwen and her husband live locally.

Ed Morris

Ed began writing seriously while living in Australia. Returning to the UK in 1968, life got in the way and writing ceased. He returned to writing in 1989 with stories for children and had the privilege of reading them to children at their school.

Ed's main genres have been poetry and children's stories, although now, after joining the creative writing group at Whittlesey, he is keen to expand his horizons, Fugu being his first true effort.

Cathy Cade

Cathy is a former librarian who began writing in retirement. She has yet to find her genre but mostly writes short stories with an occasional deviation into rhyming verse.

Her stories and verses have appeared in both print and online anthologies and magazines, including 'Scribble', 'To Hull and Back Short Stories', 'Writer's Forum', 'People's Friend', 'Flash Fiction Magazine', 'Fractured Fiction Anthology II', and 'Writing Magazine'.

Her books, *A Year Before Christmas*, *Witch Way and other ambiguous stories*, *The Godmother, Jay and Robin; Five for Silver* and *Pond People*, are available from Amazon.

Find Cathy online at www.cathy-cade.com

Acknowledgments

Now all that's left to say is a big *Thank You* to all those who have made this book possible. That's all our Wordsmiths who have turned up, sometimes in appalling Fen weather, even on days when we had no nibbles to tempt them, and the heating was broken so we wrote with stiff fingers.

Thanks to all those who have re-read, re-edited and rewritten their contributions and to Wendy, Val C and Hilary for their hours of proofreading.

Thanks again to group leader Henry and before him, Wendy who started Whittlesey Wordsmiths. And to Cathy who puts it all back together when it inevitably falls apart, as well as producing endless updated templates and fielding our million questions.

And, as always, thanks to our families and friends for their unfailing support and good humour, even when they were waiting to see if they would be the victim in our next misadventure.

Coastal Tales

Other Collections

from

THE WHITTLESEY WORDSMSITHS

FESTIVE STOCKING-FILLERS FROM

WHITTLESEY WORDSMITHS

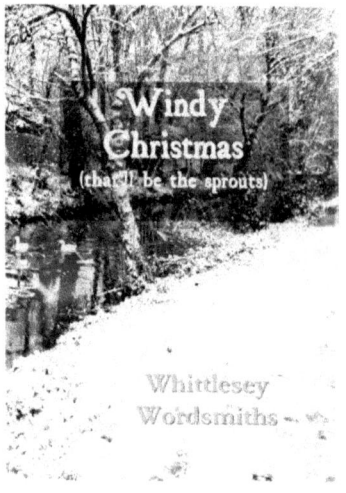

OTHER GREAT BOOKS FROM

WHITTLESEY WORDSMITHS'

AUTHORS

Coastal Tales

A memoir from Wendy

Phil's debut novel

Tessa's poems

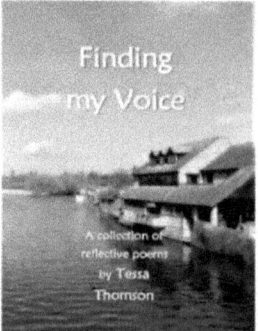

Val's limericks

All available from Amazon

From Cathy

Available from Amazon and Smashwords

~ ~ ~

From Stephen

Available from Amazon and Smashwords

Henry and Lynn Curry

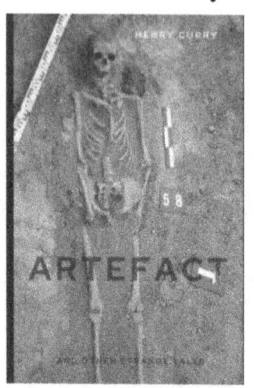

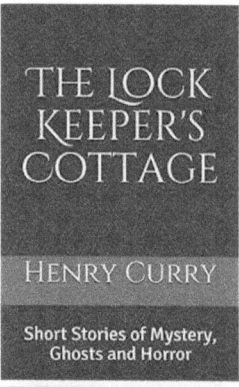
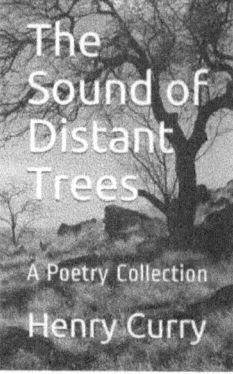

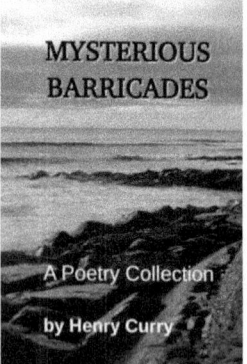

www.ingramcontent.com/pod-product-compliance
Lightning Source LLC
Chambersburg PA
CBHW070549050426
42450CB00011B/2777